The Unknown History of Islam

A Theological, Linguistic, Historical, and Sociological Study

By Sami Benjamin

Copyright © April 2013

Acknowledgments

I would like to express my deep gratitude to the following authors, philosophers, writers, and books for helping me write this book: William Shakespeare, T. S. Eliot, S. T. Coleridge, Scott Fitzgerald, Nasr Hamid Abu Zayd, Mark Twain, William C. Williams, Robert Browning, Marcel Proust, E. M. Forster, Taha Hussein, Ibn Hisham, W. H. Auden, Francis Bacon, W. B. Yeats, Uhanna Al-Dimashqui, Edgar Allan Poe, Saad Bin Mansour Bin Kammounah, Albert Camus, Avicenna, Alan Paton, Nathaniel Hawthorne, Emily Bronte, Abu Al-Farag Al-Asfahani, Chinua Achebe, Al-Farabi, John Bunyan, Hamza Kashgary, Christopher Marlowe, Joseph Conrad, Alexander Pushkin, Averroes, Abu Hayan Al-Tauheedi, Socrates, Aristotle, Plato, Naguib Mahfouz, Salman Rushdie, James Joyce, *Al-Moghny* by Ibn Kodama, *Tafseer Al-Qurtobi, Tafseer Ibn Katheer, Tafseer Al-Tabari, The Quran, Tafseer Al-Saadi, and Sahih Al-Bukhari.*

"Welcome, O life! I go to encounter for the millionth time the reality of experience and to forge in the smithy of my soul the uncreated conscience of my race.... Old father, old artificer, stand me now and ever in good stead."

James Joyce

Introduction

This book is about an actual journey into the heart of the Islamic world, Saudi Arabia. It tells of the discoveries and revelations about the history of the Middle East, Islam, and Muslims. The findings are about the theology of Islam, the language of the Quran, the history of radical Islam, and the social life of Muslims. The book presents an unprecedented analysis of the Quran and an empirical study of the psychological effect of the language of the Quran; there is also a historical and a sociological approach to understand Islam that has never been attempted before. In addition, the book exposes the goals and plans of terrorist groups such as Al-Qaeda, Boko Haram, Taliban, ISIL, Islamic Jihad, Hamas, and the Muslim Brotherhood and their followers who want to take over the world, spread Islamic Sharia law, and destroy human civilization. The author connects the dots between the early Islamic State at the time of Muhammad and modern-day terrorism and radicalism. The book also explores the beauty of literature and how it can defeat Islamic radicalism, and how literature can be used to change the rigid mindset of some radicals. The book also shows how peaceful Muslims become victims to those extremists and terrorists. It is hoped that radical Muslims would show little humbleness and some humility after they know what their religion is about and learn the truth of the Quran.

This book is a rational analysis of the past and present of the Middle East and Islam, the authenticity of the Quran, the life of Muslims under Sharia law, and the control of the clergy over the lives of Muslims, but it warns of the lurking danger of radical Islam that might jeopardize human civilization if it is not stopped immediately.

The author of this book, Sami Benjamin, was born in Iraq in 1949. He was raised as a Muslim in a Baghdad neighborhood. He moved to the United Kingdom in 1985, escaping Saddam's regime. Currently, he works in a publishing company in London since 2012. The author lives with his wife in a London suburb. He has three children and six grandchildren. The author had the privilege of the friendship of Mr. Samir Amin Kumar Abdel Latif of the Indian Publishing House in India who helped the author publish this book. The publisher, Samir Amin Kumar Abdel Latif, is an Indian national and was born in 1954 in Hyderabad, India; he lives in India and continues to reveal the truth about the Quran.

Chapter 1

In the Land of Muhammad

I lived in many Muslim countries such as Iraq, Morocco, Libya, Egypt, and Syria. However, my scholarly pursuits as a linguist and as an Islamic theologian would not be satisfactorily fruitful without living in Saudi Arabia, the cradle of Islam and the land of Waraqah Ibn Naufal, the Prophet Muhammad, Muhammad Ibn Abdel Wahab, and Osama bin Laden.

Thus, as soon as an opportunity came up in 2008, I seized on it with full force. Within few weeks, I found myself on an airplane heading to the land of Islam to teach English. A Saudi friend of mine and a former student told me in Virginia one day that Saudi Arabia is "a peaceful place, a pure place that does not know sin, greed, crime, poverty, intolerance, or hypocrisy. It is the holy land of Islam and the Quran where the Prophet Muhammad lived." My Saudi friend repeated that to me on several occasions.

When I arrived in Riyadh, the capital, the taxi driver demanded fifty dollars above the regular rate in advance. Seeing his determination and scowling face, I agreed to pay without argument. On the way to the hotel, I saw two big men with long thick beards beating up a woman and dragging her on the ground.

"These are the *Mutawe*, the religious police," the surly taxi driver explained to me. "This woman must have been doing sex things or maybe she was by herself without a man," he added. It was a very hot day in September and I was very tired after a twenty-two hour flight.

We passed by a vast barren area that extended for miles. The driver quickly noted that it was the Riyadh cemetery. There was not even a tree or any structure that was two feet high. The graves looked scary like short eerie creatures.

I was silent for few moments when I saw a large building that looked like a hotel from a distance with tiny windows and a large high wall with barbed wire around the wall.

"Is that my hotel?" I asked eagerly.

"This is the provincial prison," he said in a subdued voice.

There were mosques everywhere with very tall forbidding minarets. I looked for crosses on any of the minarets which I mistook first for church towers hoping that there would be a church or even a synagogue, but there was none.

I realized that there were more mosques per one square mile in Riyadh than people. When I arrived to the hotel, there were young boys asking for money. They grabbed one suitcase but the hotel security yelled at them and chased them away. The following day, I saw the massive courthouse at the street corner as I was leaving to see my new apartment.

Chapter Two

Literature and Islam

I went to Saudi Arabia to teach English, Arabic, and Linguistics at a college in Riyadh upon a call from an old friend I met in Virginia. His name was Tim Hallandale who said in an email that there was a vacancy open where he was working. The first class was teaching Shakespeare's *Hamlet*. There was a lot to know about how Muslims see literature in particular and Western Culture in general. The central passage of "To be or not to be" is in essence a statement that is anti-Islam, according to Muslim students.

"We humans have no choice to decide to be or not to be," one student vehemently and assertively said.

"This is completely against the teachings of our religion," another student added with a frown on his face.

I tried to explain Hamlet's existential dilemma and that his questions were philosophical, ontological, and epistemological queries rather than attempts to offend any religion. I explained that Hamlet was questioning the reasons of human agony and misery that were part of human existence and knowledge. Hamlet was only trying to seek ways to end human suffering in a philosophical argument.

"We don't care about philosophy; it's forbidden in Islam," a third student shouted.

"We exist because Allah wants us to exist," a louder voice came from another corner of the class. "We are rewarded by Allah for our suffering," he said haughtily.

I was a bit taken aback. When I finished the class, I saw Tim and called him for help and asked those students to wait and we all had a little conversation with Tim present. I was, I admit, a little shaken. Tim concurred with the students and asserted it was also anti-Christianity to express what Hamlet said. Tim was a master of resolving such issues using sarcasm and humor sometimes. As a matter of fact, students hated literature generally and poetry in particular because it is anti-Islam; and the Quran affirms, as some students told me, that in two verses where poets are described as "seducers and accompany devils." I could not find that exact description of poets in the Quran, but I found something close, though, in meaning.

The following class and to every other group I was teaching, I emphasized to students that learning is universal and eternal, religion is not; learning is right, fair and objective and for all humanity unlike religion which is limited only to its followers and it is subjective and is only for a specific purpose. Learning and knowledge benefited humanity. With all the religions we have, no religion has ever changed humanity; there are still criminals, liars, terrorists, and thugs who act in the name of their religion. There are far more murderers who killed innocents in the name of Allah and God than in the name of the devil.

Chapter Three

A Conversion to Islam Event

At the university where Tim and I worked, the main contact method was email. There were also flyers and posters to bring students and faculty attention to important events, meetings, and all other social and religious gatherings. Our email boxes were inundated daily with all sorts of messages from all over and about everything. It is difficult most of the time to notice important events, and we even missed a faculty meeting or two because of the unfiltered flow of messages that come from inside the university and from outside as well.

One day in October 2008, we noticed an unusual commotion around our campus. It was not an unusual matter to see the campus like that, but that day was different. The campus was hosting a Filipino man and an American who converted to Islam. How did I know that? Almost all those who saw me that day, asked me if I was going to "be a Muslim." My bland and insightful reply was always, "I am studying Islam to a point of complete understanding. I want to know everything before I make a decision." This answer gives them satisfaction and disappointment at the same time. Why disappointment? Because I am not in *yet*. Some ultra conservative Muslim students and faculty were keen on seeing Tim and I converting to Islam one day.

The truth was that I wanted to dig deep into the unknown realms of Islam. And I meant the things that we never knew in the West and the things that the majority of Muslims themselves do not even know about their religion. I was seriously keen on learning the truth behind that religion. I wanted to know everything. That enterprise gave me ample freedom in the Saudi society, among faculty and students to study every aspect and ask about every detail. I got some immunity to ask since my declared goal was a "complete understanding."

Before I went to Saudi Arabia, I knew already a lot about Islam; after few years in the land of Muhammad and extensive reading and investigation, I learned even more to a point of shocking discoveries that I will unfold in the next chapters of this book. I never thought I would know that much.

Tim had a different approach, perhaps more diplomatic and blunter at the same time. His cliché answer when asked if he would convert or whether he converted already was, "Islam is a great religion not worthy of someone like me." Tim's mild nature lent him immunity from aggressive proselytizing. On the other hand, my inquisitive enterprise acquired me a lot of attention and scrutiny, but I got ultimately what I was after: the truth about Islam.

***

By the time Tim and I arrived to the "Festivities Hall," we could hear a great deal of loud noises and cheers from the five-hundred-plus audience. One student proudly pointed out, almost screaming to me, that "The converts are definitely going to paradise."

"Why is that?" I asked with stifled indignation.

"They are Muslim now. Al-hamdu lillah," he said.

"Sure, of course."

The phrase "Al-hamdu lillah" means thanks to Allah or God.

***

The event started with a traditional recitation of the Quran. Everybody in the hall was silent during that recitation. Afterwards, a speaker talked about the rewards and blessings of being a Muslim and the punishment waiting for the infidels who oppose Islam or refuse to enter Islam. "Allah will punish those who do not become Muslims as Allah affirms that in the Quran;" then he recited:

"Indeed, the only religion for Allah is Islam. And those who were given the Scripture (Jews and Christians) did not differ except after knowledge had come to them - out of jealous animosity between themselves must follow Islam. And whoever disbelieves in the verses of Allah, and then indeed, Allah is swift in taking appropriate measures (to punish them)." (Aal-Omran, 19)

The speaker added that there was great punishment waiting for those who follow other religions. The speaker said that in a loud vociferous voice. Tim turned his head half way towards me. I nodded a half nod in return.

Then, the Filipino man started talking about his journey to find Islam and the wonder of the Quran, and how he sinned in the past a lot and only his work "buddies" in Saudi Arabia directed him to Islam at which point he felt that it was the best religion for him. I noticed that the Filipino never looked up or towards the eager audience. He never maintained eye contact with the audience for even two seconds at a time. He looked down on the table and would reach for his bottle of water every few minutes to take a sip and release a sigh. It seemed to me he was not even breathing regularly because he was in some kind of agony or regret over something.

Next was an African American who worked as an airline mechanic and ended up living and working in Saudi Arabia for the Saudi Airlines. He told the audience of his early life in Saint Louis, Missouri. He told them of the harsh life he had as a youngster in the ghetto. He then elaborated on his teenage years and the ease of getting drugs and prostitutes. At that moment, the audience hummed, not in anger or disgust, but I can say there was some approval in their humming. Then, he spoke about his first wife who did not like the idea of converting to Islam and his second wife who accepted Islam but when she went home for a visit to see her family in Baltimore, she never came back. He also stressed the charm of the Quran on him. At that time, we started to look at our cell phones to check the time. I wanted to leave.

After the event, some faculty and students approached us and asked me the usual boring questions such as:

"What do you think?" one student asked me.

"This is great. I never thought I'll see someone from Missouri here in Saudi Arabia," I said facetiously.

Tim was two steps ahead of me and would look behind every few steps. He was smiling all the time.

Such conversions meant a lot to radical Muslims. This event was very significant as it explained the psychological triumph that radical Muslims are seeking. A conversion to Islam is a great victory and a sign from Allah that Islam is marching on.

Chapter Four

Faith VS Reason

Religious life in Saudi Arabia is so peculiar. One is under watch at all times from the religious police, called *Mutawe*. Moreover, one is being evaluated and judged by others depending on one's religiosity and the amount of religious practice; the more, the better one is. The more religiosity one manifests, the more ethical one is assumed to be in Islamic countries; the more outward show of faith (such as a long thick beard and wife and daughters all covered up), the more trustworthy one is; the more Quran one uses in his or her speech or conversation, the more pious one is. The more one goes to the mosque, the better Muslim one is or assumed to be.

In this atmosphere, one comes under tremendous pressure. In a court of law, the length of one's beard lends credibility to his testimony in proportion to that beard's length and vice versa. One's eligibility for a job is decided by one's Islamic knowledge, and not by one's technical expertise. A young woman's or a young man's eligibility and chances of marriage are determined by her or his pious utterances and phrases used in a conversation. One's chances to be promoted in the workplace increase immensely with one's outward reverence to Islamic traditions. People then have no choice but show faith in all and every way possible. That has bred a lot of hypocrisy, deception, and insincerity.

Hypocrisy, deception, and insincerity are inevitable for some to survive in such an environment. "Cunning" might be the weapon that a Saudi friend used to describe the survival technique of those who come under such pressure.

During my stay in Saudi Arabia, I gained the trust of one Saudi colleague named Yehya. He was a professor in the Arabic Department. He was an associate professor of Arabic literature. My love and appreciation of Arabic literature had been doubled when I listened to him explaining some great literary works such as Arabic ninth century poetry or modern novels. He was a real scholar. I also shared with him some English masterpieces that he heard about but never got a chance to approach. He was very happy and ecstatic to get to know some of the great English and American poems, novels, and plays. We read together a large number of excerpts from both literatures and discussed their content and artistic beauty and the miracles of such literary splendor of those texts we shared.

He trusted me so much that he confided to me that he is not practicing Islam as he found out that Islam is more likely to be fake than true. I confirmed his findings and, secretly, we shared many findings and conclusions about Muhammad and the Quran. We had illuminating revelations about the many palpable contradictions in the Quran; and if Allah is true, then he would not craft the Quran with such inconsistencies and incongruities. Therefore, the Quran cannot be the work of a higher being but rather the work of an individual, at best, an educated writer. We talked a lot about Waraqah Ibn Naufal and his role in the establishment of Islam. We also talked about Uthman's Quran and the many versions of the Quran that were in circulation after the death of Muhammad in 632 CE.

The professor told me that there were so many other Saudis who had the same knowledge about Islam and its awkward start and how fake it was. The point was that no one could publicly speak about this. As a result, many people have to live a double life for fear of terrible retribution and certain execution for blasphemy.

It was an act of fate that changed matters for my colleague, professor Yehya. One day, his only son was hit by a car near his home, and the son died instantly. When I saw him five days later at the college, he was so haggard and so emaciated. He avoided looking at me the whole day. He basically avoided me altogether. A week later, I reached for him and tried to tell him that it was an accident that could happen to anyone, but he shook his head in rejection of that description of what happened.

Two weeks later, professor Yehya said to me it was Allah's punishment for him because he did not have faith in Allah. He cited some Quran verses that promise punishment for those who do not follow Allah's commandments. Another colleague, named professor Shahab, also from the Arabic department supported his claim that Allah punishes the wrong doers and rewards the faithful and the followers of Allah. He cited:

"And for those who disbelieve, there will be Hell. Death is not granted for them so if they die, it is mercy and comfort for them, nor will its torment be allayed for them. Thus We punish every ungrateful one (permanent torture in fire without death)." (Fatir, 36)

Then he added another verse:

"But those who believe and do righteous deeds - those are the admitted ones to Paradise; they will abide therein eternally."

(Al-Baqara, 82)

***

I tried to give a more rational explanation and mentioned that it was an accident just waiting to happen. They rebutted that there was no such a thing called accident, but it was all Allah's design and plan set forth to punish and reward, nothing else. Professor Shahab was the kind of man who was very pious and "oozing" religion all over, so to speak. He had the longest and thickest beard I have ever seen. His forehead had such a huge, very dark and rough spot of skin from the frequent hitting of the ground when he kneels down in praying. He was in every measure the ultimate Muslim fundamentalist anywhere to be found or seen. He was so hard on himself during Ramadan that he would fast two hours longer than required by the Quran. He would only break his fast after Al-Ishaa prayer, the last prayer of the day which is way late at night. He would pray much more than anyone else, and fast five months during the year, five times more than requested. He always boasted that "Allah will reward him and his family, with Allah's mercy and will only, with the best rewards for his *Taqwa* (or piety)."

The first brush with him, a month after my arrival to Saudi Arabia, was not a very pleasant one. He gave me during a faculty meeting a book about Islamic ways of exorcising the devil. I am a person who did not care much about devils or angels. I only care about life and lead a normal, simple life to help fellow human beings, so I was not impressed about that book. Apparently, he did not like my indifference to the book. I looked at the book and just handed it back to him with my left hand. That was a terrible mistake.

Professor Shahab gave me a lengthy reproach about using the right hand and how that was the core of Islamic behavior.

"The devil lives in the left hand; Allah blessed the right hand; that's why we should use the right hand only," he yelled.

"Great! This is also a Jewish tradition," I said. Clearly that was a big mistake on my part to mention anything Jewish. He roared and his face literally twisted in a scary way. So I went back quickly to my usual routine.

"Well, I have been created with two hands and definitely if the left hand was an evil one, Allah would have given two right hands, or just one right hand," I rebutted.

Apparently, that did not help either. He started to quote a verse from the Quran that described the evil of the left hand and the blessings of the right hand. It was a moment of extreme aggravation and I left as soon as the opportunity presented itself. By the standards of Islam, "The right hand is good." I remember one day giving money to a cashier in the supermarket using my left hand and I received the same hee-haw as well.

Professor Shahab was undoubtedly so impressive in his faith that I felt he was overdoing it. Definitely, he was very faithful in Allah and the Quran, a very strict person in his belief. He learned the whole Quran by rote when he was five years old. He knows everything in the Quran and its interpretation and the very specific circumstances of every verse. He would not accept any argument against Islam. He was so dedicated to Islam that he would do anything to stop its enemies; he affirmed many times in a very aggressive manner, that he "Would kill anyone who would raise doubts about Islam."

Professor Shahab would interrupt his classes to pray. He would teach more Quran and Islam in his classes than the material he was supposed to teach. He was a professor of poetry, but he always spent the class time attacking poetry and poets, and he would choose only in his syllabi religious poems that glorify Islam and Muslims. He never showed a taste for literary aesthetics; instead he affirmed to his students that literature and art in general were corrupt because they distract people from the word of Allah.

I saw professor Yehya on a regular basis as his office was not far from mine. I frequented his office at times, looked into his bookcase and tried to see if he got new books or volumes. I never dared to talk about any subjects related to the Quran authenticity or Muhammad's commission from Allah any more as we used to before the death of his son which he attributed to his lack of complete faith and pious following of Allah.

On the other hand, Professor Shahab performed the Hajj every year since he was ten years old. An adult Muslim is required to perform at least one Hajj trip in a life time, but he performed it "forty-one times," he proudly said. Professor Shahab also performed Omrah, the lesser Hajj, which is done between one Hajj and another. He mentioned confidently that he would go for Omrah at least three times a year. Most Muslims I knew did Hajj or Omrah just once in their life time; many more never had the chance to do either and many more do not have the intention to do either because it is very costly and very exhausting as well. However, professor Shahab always boasted that he loved Allah and Allah loved him a lot.

"With Allah's mercy and will, I am blessed and loved by Allah and my family is safe by Allah's mercy and will and they can have peace and prosperity for I am an obedient servant of Allah," he said to me in a very assured voice one time and asked me to be a servant of Allah, too, so I "get the rewards and avoid the punishment."

"Sure," I said curtly.

"Brother Sam, we will start next week during the spring break a caravan to Mecca for Omrah and we expect you, then, if you want to be a true follower of Allah to accompany us, may Allah bless you," he said with full eye contact. What ticked me was that he called me "brother," not the usual "Doctor Sam" or "Professor Sam." I only called him and others by either "professor" or "doctor." Now I felt my status had changed. I mused and felt a little amused and sarcastic.

"You can convince Brother Tim to come too," he added.

"I don't really know about Doctor Tim, but I have plans for the break. I need to work on some late research that is due soon. I'm so sorry," I said firmly.

"But Brother Tim suggested you might be interested," he said.

"I really appreciate Tim's word for me, but I will thank him a lot the moment I see him," I said restraining a burst of laughter.

"I have a big SUV and I and my two sons are going and you are welcome by the mercy and will of Allah, we will be blessed for this Omrah," he coaxed.

"Next time and I'll try to convince professor Tim to be with us, next year maybe, next year for sure if we feel like going. Sure another time, another time," I said, a little embarrassed as it was the last thing to expect was to be asked to go to Mecca for Omrah. It was funny and unusual even thinking about it.

"Remember I have a big SUV and there is plenty of space for you and Brother Tim," he repeated.

"Next time, next year if things are OK with us and you, next year; don't worry," I said firmly but still embarrassed.

By the end of March, there is that break. Spring here in Saudi Arabia is like a very hot summer. Temperature was around 105 already. I was awakened in the morning by phone on a Sunday about 11:00 am to hear professor Yehya loud but indistinct voice. He tried to tell me that professor Shahab and his two sons died when the right front tire of his SUV exploded and the truck just rolled about eight times according to witnesses. The truck was described as a result of the high speed rollover as a mangled piece of metal and there were no survivors.

I never talked to professor Yehya again until one time about a month later; he approached me with a smothered smile and said, "Maybe if you went with the late professor Shahab to Mecca, he might have been alive today."

"Maybe, maybe. It is all an accident, you know," I said in a low voice.

He nodded in agreement and smiled confidently. He sent me later that week a new issue of a selection of Arabic poetry.

Chapter Five

Muslims

This chapter is about Muslims and the different types of Muslims. Essentially, there is the extremist, fundamentalist type that wants to spread Sharia Islamic law in the whole world regardless of the means and methods to be used to achieve this goal. The second type is the true peaceful, spiritual Muslim who seeks a quiet life without strife or violence. Unlike the first type, a peaceful Muslim will not emphasize the appearances of head and face cover or the beard and all those outward signs. Moreover, a peaceful Muslim is the one that integrates unreservedly into his or her new Western culture. These are some of the quick clues that set them apart. However, there are deeper, hard to detect clues that mark extreme radicals, namely, the keenness to use violence any time and the determination to make every person living on this planet follow the religion of Islam in the way they see it and make Sharia the sole law governing the whole world.

Therefore, names such as "Ahmad" or "Muhammad" are not enough to tell if a person is an extremist Muslim. There are in fact many people who are moderate, peace loving Muslims named "Ahmad" or "Muhammad." Moreover, there are those who are not even Muslim at all with these names. One has to find out the extent of a person's intentions to use violence to spread Sharia law and that is the cutoff line.

Luckily, many Muslims are peace-loving people. The word "many" is a relative term. It can be anything from 91% to 99% depending on the community or country. However, one percent of the population being extremists can still turn a society into violence and chaos in the name of Allah and Sharia. We must in the West hail the moderate and keep an eye on the extremists. We must always remember that the war against Islamic radicalism and violence is a war that we cannot lose. The fate of humanity and civilization is at stake. It is not a war on drugs or leftist guerrillas. No. It is a war of humanity against the destruction of humanity.

Islamic radicals and terrorists have done the following:

1- In the past, they destroyed the achievements and treasures of many civilizations, namely, the Ancient Egyptian and Coptic civilizations in Egypt (Muslim radical invaders actually burned down the Great Library of Alexandria), the Sassanid Civilization in Persia, all the ancient civilizations of the Mediterranean, all central Asia and south east Asia civilizations, the Byzantine, the Anatolian, the Assyrian, the Canaanite, the Greek, the Chinese, the Indian, and many more civilizations were claimed as victims of the radical Islamic invasions and plundering. For example, the Dark Ages in Europe were the result of Islamic terror campaigns on Europe during the eighth century (AD) and after. Radical Muslims invaded the shores of southern Europe and sank commercial ships sailing the Mediterranean. European affluent trade was immensely slowed. The result was sinking Europe into atrocious economic collapse, political chaos, and cultural demise. The Muslim terrorist raids on all southern shores of Europe and into the heart of Europe from the east through Turkey, Bulgaria, and all the way to the gates of Vienna and from the west via Spain and up to the borders of France had the biggest devastating effect on the world in general and Europe in particular. At the same time, the Silk Road was cut off and all the peoples who lived along the Silk Road were forced to convert to Islam. As a matter of fact, the Silk Road itself became a highway to send radicals to plunder all the riches of the East and the West while depriving all the regions along the Silk Road from China to Europe of all trade and industry prosperity that they enjoyed before.

2- Radical Muslims and terrorists have slowed down all advancement and progress of all the nations they set foot in. Because of those radicals, Islamic countries sadly live in poverty, disease, underdevelopment, and chaos. Not to mention the setbacks in democracy, and abject failure in scientific and technological achievement. All because of Muslim terrorists and radicals.

Furthermore, radicals, mainly Muslim Brotherhood members, since 1947, have maintained unjustly and unreasonably that Jerusalem is theirs even though the Quran itself states that Mecca, not Jerusalem, as the first holy house of Allah. Terrorists irrationally started five wars and caused the death of more than a million people and caused stagnation to world economy several times and triggered many other proxy wars and created tension in the world because of Jerusalem even though the Quran unequivocally states:

"Indeed, the first House established for mankind

was that at Mecca - blessed and guidance for the whole world." (Aal-Omran, 96)

Moreover, there are two verses in the Quran in which Allah indisputably grants the Holy Land to the Children of Israel.

"O my people (Israelites) enter the Holy Land which Allah has granted to you and do not turn back [from fighting in Allah's cause] and [thus] become losers." (Al-Maeda, 21)

This is confirmed again:

"And We said after the Pharaoh to the Children of Israel, "Dwell in the land, and when there comes the promise of the Hereafter, We will bring you forth in [one] gathering." (Al-Israa, 104)

Palestinians definitely have historical rights, but Muslims do not have religious rights in the Holy Land.

Nothing said so far should bias anyone against Muslims in general. In no way, we as individuals can decide against a person because of his name or her Arab-looking face. Furthermore, a Muslim and a good person are not antithetical. No. Nothing in this book should be interpreted in this way. To repeat, the whopping majority of Muslims who are just like the rest of us are truly kind and peace-loving human beings. This book is only warning against radicals and terrorists who constitute small percentage of the total Muslim body. Unfortunately, that small percentage is about two hundred million Jihadists and terrorists. A number that is bigger than all the armies of the world. In addition and more sinisterly, these terrorists are strategically spread all over the world, in France, Brazil, Mali, Egypt, Russia, Belgium, Syria, and the United states, to mention a few countries. This is a fact the world must deal with courageously. They conveniently work under different umbrella organizations such as Al-Qaeda, ISIL (under formation by Saudi Arabia, Turkey, and Qatar), and the Muslim Brotherhood.

Chapter Six

Islamophobia

The so-called "Islamophobia" is a ruse used by radicals in Europe and North America to stop the West from scrutinizing radical Muslims. However, terrorists and radicals always try to browbeat anyone who would dare to complain about anything radical, from strange behavior to terrorism. Some might say "What's wrong! It's their way of life." No, it is not a way of life if it does not fit in with our Western way of life and values that we and our ancestors have had for centuries before any radicals came to Europe or the Americas. Peaceful Muslims who are the sweeping majority of Muslims are definitely welcome to their new home, but not Muslim terrorists and radicals.

The term 'Islamophobia' is, however, a misnomer that is semantically incorrect. A 'phobia' denotes an irrational fear of something. We are not afraid of radical Islam as so much as threatened, sickened, and offended by its violence and stone-age backwardness; any fear of radical Islam is genuine and well-founded. Muslim radicals' bigoted views and myopic intent to rule earth with Sharia is bloodcurdling and a real threat to human civilization.

Radicals would try to force their values and traditions on others callously. They would force their neighbors to cover their heads and faces otherwise they taunt them for not being modest. Radical teachers would try to make their students from other religions pray according to their radicalized brand of Islam. In many cases, radical Muslims' victims are just other peaceful Muslims who want to lead a decent life.

Extremists usually manifest a certain amount of radicalism contingent upon two factors:

1- Their percentage in the total population in a country.

2- The degree of their leaders' extremism.

This means that radicals use the percentage of innocent Muslims in a country to their advantage and ratchet up the amount of rage and violence. For example, in Pakistan (98% Muslim) radicals intensify the tension over any incident they consider offensive to the prophet Muhammad, while in Italy (only 2% Muslim) rage and violence manifested by radicals over the same incident would be low in comparison.

***

So what happens if Muslims are fewer than 3% in a country? In countries such as Italy, Canada, the United States, and Belgium where peaceful Muslims constitute that small minority, the radicals and extremists hiding amongst them are always preparing for violence and would resort to terrorism when they feel like it; they would fake a life of peace and tolerance, but they would continue to harbor grudge and vengeance. They would secretly treat people in their neighborhood and at work, for example, who happen to be Christian or Jewish as infidels. They would also hold secret meetings and curse the government and the people of the host country; they would never thank the host country or its people for having them in that country; they would never express appreciation for being there, but rather they would think of the time when they would have their revenge against the host people. They would never be proud of their host country if, for example, its national team wins a game in FIFA World Cup or Olympics. They would gloat over any mishap that befalls their American or Italian neighbor; they would crow over any national disaster that befalls the host country. They will never be part of the fabric of that country or ever consider themselves nationals of that country that kindly harbor them. These radicals would even resent that other peaceful Muslims, who are usually the majority of the Muslim community, are not sharing their hate towards the host country.

In a country where Muslims are under 10% of the population but more than 3%, as it is the case in the Netherlands, France and England, one would expect more outward manifestation of grudge from radicals and extremists against the members of their society and would resort to terrorism and street rage whenever an opportunity presents itself. They maintain more visible presence and more boldness in criticizing people of other religions. They would demand more rights such as building Mosques in places that are not usually set for buildings, demand special holidays (I'm not talking about religious holidays) to be observed by everyone in the community, and try to force others including other peaceful Muslims, to adapt to their extreme brand of Islam. There are more veiled women in the streets and far more women with their heads covered than one should expect to see in a Western country. These radicals would even threaten other peaceful Muslims to follow in their footsteps. These radicals force their wives and daughters to cover their heads and faces. There are many cases documented in police reports where women and girls as young as ten who were forced to do so.

When their percentage in a country is a little under 25%, one would expect daily rampage and mayhem by radicals and terrorists, against the will of the peaceful Muslim majority in the community, as it is the case in India and the Philippines; there would be open conflict with other social and religious groups. They would try to impose openly by using violence their Sharia and their way of life on everybody else including innocent peaceful Muslims. Jihad calls are loudly heard and grating tension becomes a daily routine.

When Muslims reach a percentage near 50%, radicals and the extremists amongst them, and against the will of the peaceful Muslim majority in the community, would try to seize power, terrorize everyone else, force Sharia (Islamic law) and would not hesitate to wipe out other groups. This is the case in Nigeria, Ethiopia, Mali, and Bosnia.

In all the examples mentioned so far, i.e. from 1% to 50%, extremists and radicals would try to push their agenda into the fabric of their societies, disregarding the rights of the majority. They would even try to push for legal and social rights not even available for the majority. Extremists and radicals would cry foul for anything that remotely touches them. They want to throw their weight around while remaining untouchable. They would not take any criticism, but rather they would consider it a barbaric attack on their religion causing great embarrassment to the sweeping majority of the peaceful Muslim community.

If the Muslim population exceeds 90%, as it is the case in Egypt, Libya, Afghanistan, Somalia, Yemen, Saudi Arabia, Indonesia, Pakistan, Tunis, Sudan, and many other countries, one would expect open and unabashed recruitment of terrorists; animosity to the West is unrestrained and unabated. Radicals and terrorists would pray openly for the destruction of the West. They would call for Allah's curse to annihilate Christians and Jews and people of other religions. They would blame all their problems, ineptitude, and inefficiency on the West and weave these problems into the myth of conspiracy theories that the West is trying to destroy or weaken them. These countries are either ruled by extremist leaders who believe in the monopoly of Islamic law over any other law as it is the case in Saudi Arabia, Egypt (only under Muslim Brotherhood rule in 2012/2013; a popular uprising in 6/30/2013 removed the radical Muslim president and restored secular rule), and Sudan. Manifestly, the extremist culture of Wahabi Islam rules the streets, the minds, the hearts, and thoughts of the terrorists and extremists as it is the case in Saudi Arabia, Yemen, Sudan, Pakistan, Tunis, Egypt, Somalia, Chechnya, Afghanistan, and Syria, to name a few. In either case, whether it is the rulers or the people and their extreme culture of intolerance, one would find blatant persecution of other minority religions. No liberal thoughts are allowed; women are completely marginalized; liberal education, the arts, and technology are frowned upon and society remains underdeveloped.

Some countries, East and West, have started to implement some measures that would protect and preserve the local culture of its residents, and the values of the people who have lived there for thousands of years against the whims of extremists. For example, Switzerland decided not to allow high minarets for mosques in some places where high structures are not supposed to be built at all. It is a measure to prevent the obtrusive change of the landscape that the Swiss have always seen in their country. However, extremists decided to build high structures only to "spite the Swiss government and the people." The Swiss tried to protect their country and the Swiss have the right to keep it the way they like it. What was the extremists' reaction? They cried Islamophobia. However, the majority of peaceful Muslims in the community felt very embarrassed by the extremists' unreasonable demands.

Similarly, France and the Netherlands took some legal measures to stop women from covering their faces in public places. There is a security legitimate component in that measure. There have been numerous crimes done by some people hiding their faces and simply could not be identified. Besides, covering the face is not and has never been a European way of life. Europeans are simply trying to protect their security and preserve their traditions and native cultures.

Myanmar in south central Asia has been under continuous threat from some Muslim terrorist groups that wreaked havoc on the country, and the government had to take some action to stop that attack on its people. All are legitimate measures to keep law and order that Muslim Wahabi terrorists have no respect for. No one should blame a society for stopping an attack by terrorists on its fabric and its way of life in the name of Islamophobia.

Chapter Seven

The Rise of Radical Islam

Turkey or rather the Ottoman Empire was the last seat of the Islamic Empire; the last caliphate was held by Ottoman Turkish sultans. However, the first secular president of Turkey, Kemal Atatürk in 1924 abolished the caliphate as a consequence of the Ottoman Empire's defeat in World War I. That marked the end of the Islamic Empire ruled by Caliphs. A caliph basically means "a successor of the Prophet Muhammad." After the fall of the Islamic empire officially and the end of the Islamic Caliphate, Muslims reaction was two-pronged. There was a shock and call for Islamic revival on one hand. There was a sense of subdued surrender on the other.

For a while, the second tendency ruled the scene. The majority of Muslims around the world just minded their own life. For about sixty years, from about 1918 till 1978, radical Islam was not an international issue. The year 1918 marked the end of World War I. The Year 1978 marked the start of the Islamic revolution in Iran which culminated in the establishment of the Islamic Republic of Iran in 1979 (the same year the Soviet Union invaded Afghanistan and the rise of the extremist Mujahedeen). No one heard of political Islam during that sixty-year period from 1918 to 1978. Islam was not a threat in any way to international peace. The reason was very simple: Both the West and Muslims had a common enemy: The Soviet Union and Communism, its ideology. The eighties of the twentieth century came with good and bad news for the West. The Soviets were implicated in a costly war in Afghanistan; also the eighties witnessed the fall of the Soviet Union. However, radical Islam took roots everywhere in the world and it suddenly became the new threat to the civilized world. The world was taken off guard. Radical political Islam has been growing fast since then and there is no hope or strategy to curb it any time soon. Radical Muslims' victory in Afghanistan was a great boost for them as they further entertained the thought that if they could defeat one empire (the Soviet Union), then why not defeat the other empire, i.e., the Western world. It seemed to many observers that the rise of radical Islam was inevitable. It was natural for extremists to fill in the ideological vacuum left by the demise of Communism. The surge in radical violent Islam and its terror during the 1990's and the 2000's have stemmed from thirteen conditions and reasons:

- First, the lack of a strategy to handle extremist radical Islam from day one by any Western powers.

- Secondly, the West had technically got accustomed to violent Islam during the war of the Mujahedeen in Afghanistan against the Soviet Union. The United States and Western Europe actually armed, trained, financed, and supported the extremists during their war against the Soviet Union. In other words, the West encouraged and tolerated radical Islam.

- Thirdly, the West in a way felt indebted to the Mujahedeen for a while, a long while, for their role in bringing down the Soviet Union.

- Fourthly, the United States made some crucial mistakes such as siding with one warlord in Afghanistan against another and ignored the fact that they were all tribesmen driven by rivalry and greed.

- Fifth, the West has clearly underestimated the radicals' hidden goals and plans, which were basically to spread radical Islam all over the world. The United States and Western Europe had little thought of the extent of radicals' aspirations and dreams of taking over the world.

- Sixth, the West, namely the United States, treated the Mujahedeen as peers and as statesmen. In fact, those Mujahedeen became the troops of Al-Qaeda soon after the end of the war against the Soviet Union. The Mujahedeen were no more than radical Muslims for hire. The warlords, i.e., the Mujahedeen leaders were tribesmen who traded in drugs and weapons decades before and after the Soviet Union invasion of Afghanistan. However and ironically, they received the unduly highest honors and credit from the West.

- Seventh, it seems without doubt now that Muslim extremists in Afghanistan and elsewhere had a plan to fill in the vacuum left by the fall of the Soviet Union and boldly demanded a share in world affairs; the West did not have a plan of its own to fill in the gap left by the Soviet Union or how to counter the demands of the radicals.

- Eighth, the United States has shown a lot of smugness and utter complacency when they treat radical Muslims whether they are from Saudi Arabia, Egypt, or the Mujahedeen warlords. American officials have no way to psych out radical Muslims and their shrewdness. American officials keep forgetting that Afghani warlords are no more than tribesmen who are seeking victory in all tribal rivalry. Wahabi Saudi and Muslim Brotherhood Egyptian dictators, for example, are master survivors who want to keep their clutch on power the longest time possible and, therefore, they know how to appease, pacify, and cajole the United States while hiding their real motives. Those dictators know how to use soft, silky foreign policy; they are slick and resourceful and know how to manipulate the West for their benefit. Moreover, the same dictators use another shrewd tactic: investment. They pump their countries' money into American and European markets and thus become major players in Western economy. It is not surprising to know that Saudis are investing more than eight hundred billion dollars in major American companies alone; also, those dictators buy Western products even though they do not need them as a way of bribery to those Western governments. The Saudis in particular contract services and buy products from companies where major players in American politics such as senators and federal government officials have invested in stocks and shares. A very clear example was when the Saudi government decided to buy civilian airplanes from Boeing for the amount of twenty billion dollars in the nineties which saved Boeing from bankruptcy but helped many members of the Congress keep their finances in great shape. This method of indirect bribery proved to be effective, legal, and legitimate, but the danger is that it allows radical Muslim regimes to creep into our Western lives and interests. Worst of all is that radicals who are part of Al-Qaeda and followers of Wahabism try to win the West over by striking alliances (a game they play well) against a third party, e.g. a Saddam-like leader or Bashar Al-Assad. The radicals try even to win Israel over. But they have a strategy which is win now and strike later. They try to get legitimacy and recognition to spread their Wahabi ideology while creeping into Western life smoothly and under our noses.

- Ninth, the only strategy the West had was a policy of containment; a tactic of ingratiating and humoring warlords and radical dictators in the Muslim world as in Afghanistan, Saudi Arabia, Egypt (under radical President Morsi), and elsewhere. The West is so naïve to think they are using radicals for their benefit; the fact is that radicals are using the West for their benefit and even making the West feel good about it.

- Tenth, in the 1990's and 2000's, the United States and the West obsessed over Saddam Hussein too much for no reason and wasted a lot of energy and resources. Meanwhile, radical Islam has been growing steadily and adding millions of extremist followers every year.

- Eleventh, one of the biggest mistakes that helped radical Islam to grow was that the United States failed to accommodate and adapt to changes in the international arena. The United States foreign policy is very stiff and lacks flexibility to absorb sudden changes in the Muslim world. For example, The United States declared that it would support the so called "Arab Spring." The United States has not realized that the "Arab Spring" is producing more radical regimes and foot soldiers for terrorism every day. The only reaction now on the part of the United States is to watch and wait (or try to win them over) to see what will happen next. So, smugness turned into apathy. Complacency became indifference par excellence.

- Twelfth, the 1980's, 1990's, and 2000's had winners, namely, the radical regimes of Qatar, Turkey, Iran and Saudi Arabia. Furthermore, in the 2010's, the radical leaders of the

Muslim brotherhood of countries such as Egypt and Tunis rose to power and became a beacon for more extremists to follow suit. Islamic radical ideology is winning so far. Qatar and Turkey, in particular, play a grave role in helping radical Muslims (they are grouping terrorists under a new name called ISIL) to destabilize secular regimes. Strangely, the West seems comfortable with (or rather in cahoots with) Qatar's and Turkey's vicious agenda and the West is failing again to see the possible terrible outcome in the long run. Every win for radicals reverberates loudly throughout the Muslim world as a testimony from Allah. Radicals believe they are near taking over the world and impose their radical brand of Islam. It is a prophecy that every radical Muslim is entitled to achieve in order to win Allah's greatest rewards. Every time there is a conversion to Islam, for example, radicals hail that as a step towards realizing Allah's promise. Every time the West is hit by a natural disaster, they hail this as a sign of the end of the West. On the other hand, when a disaster hits them, they see it as a test from Allah of their endurance and patience for which they will be ultimately rewarded. Biologically, they have calculated their majority to be achieved in the world by another forty years; the last forty years saw a great rise in the population of radicals. They expect their population to double in the next forty years.

- Thirteenth, the West is still clinging to cold-war era mentality when it comes to dealing with progressive enlightened elements in the Muslim world. The West is still wary of seculars or socialists in Muslim countries and refuses to deal with them and prefers to embrace Muslim radicals as is the case, for example, in Syria, Egypt, and Tunis.

There is no doubt that the West bears full responsibility for the rise of radical Islam. Radical Islam seems inevitable unless the West makes a move now. A drastic move.

Chapter Eight

Islamic Inquisitions and the Denigration of other Religions:

Heinous Crimes against Humanity

From day one of Islam, there were many attempts to stop the new religion. Many saw it as a disruption of their lives. The way of life in Mecca where Islam first appeared was far from a place suitable for a new religion. The atmosphere and the general disposition of the city and its inhabitants were not the right place by any extreme imagination for a new faith.

The city of Mecca was a trade hub between the Levantine in the north and Yemen and Abyssinia (modern day Ethiopia) in the south. The city was also, besides being a commercial center, a cultural center. Poets from all over Arabia would converge for their annual, semiannual and quarterly poetry reading and competitions. It was also a tourist attraction for people to go and relax or meet others. Mecca was also a religious destination for Jews, Christians and non-believers. There were in and around Mecca the biggest Jewish and Christian concentrations in all of Arabia. Everybody was happy in that city that never knew conflict until Islam seized upon it one day in 610 AD.

Muhammad's new religion simply disrupted the way of daily life of the inhabitants and visitors of Mecca. There was a fierce movement of resisting Muhammad. Muhammad's uncle, Abd Al-Uzza (d. 624 AD) and his wife, Umm Jamil, or Arwa, were among the first to put a stiff resistance against Muhammad and his new religion. Abd Al-Uzza and his wife were very refined people in Mecca; they were very polite and decent residents who did not like the disruption of their life and their activities as business owners and sponsors of the arts. The result was terrible for them. Muhammad and his followers launched a terror campaign against the couple; it started with a smear campaign and turned into a series of physical attacks on the couple.

The couple was made an example of to intimidate anyone else who would have thought of opposing Islam. They died in poverty and humiliation after they were very prosperous people in Mecca. The defamation campaign went as far as crafting a whole chapter in the Quran (Al-Masad) to denounce the man and his wife. Many more people had faced the same fate and even worse consequences for just questioning the authenticity of the new religion, Islam. All sorts of intimidation, clandestine harm, and covert damage tactics and methods of persecution were used by Muhammad and his followers to silence their critics and opponents.

After Muhammad's death, many sighed in relief thinking that the age of terror was over. But they were wrong; they were very wrong. Muhammad's successor, the first caliph of the Muslims was Abu Bakr (b. 573 - d. 634 AD). He launched the biggest inquisition in the history of Arabia; it was an act of religious cleansing against anyone, group, tribe, or people who did not follow the rules and teachings of Islam. He started a methodological and fierce campaign of religious cleansing, also called "Riddah Wars."

During his two-year rule as caliph (632-634 CE), Abu Bakr killed so many people in such a short time and took more spoils than in any other span of two years in Islamic history. He invaded all Arabia, from Yemen and Oman, to present day Emirates (called Bahrain then). He even sent forces to Syria and Iraq and conquered its people and forced them to convert to Islam. It was the biggest inquisition of its time. If one individual, a tribe, or a group of people were not Muslim or not about to convert unconditionally to Islam, death and confiscation of property were the immediate consequences.

In lands beyond Abu Bakr's reach, those who did not surrender to Islam and converted, emissaries were sent threatening that they would lose either their lives, property, or to pay Jizyah (tribute money or tax). In the conquered areas, many Christian churches and Jewish temples were plundered and destroyed during that period of Islamization of the land. In Yemen, for example, Jews had to escape to Ethiopia; those who could not escape pretended to convert to Islam to avoid death or loss of property, or both. In Palestine and Syria, historical Churches were used as make-shift Muslim soldiers' quarters, but finally confiscated and turned into mosques.

Another atrocity committed by Muhammad and finished by Abu Bakr was to wipe out Jews and Christians in Arabia. Mecca and its suburbs and all the way up to Medina before Islam had a total of eleven thousand Jews and Eight thousand Christians. By the time Abu Bakr died, there was not a single Jew or Christian alive in Mecca or Medina or around Arabia. The Quran was changed to accommodate for the new orders. Uthman, the third caliph, made drastic interpolations in the Quran to justify religious cleansing. He embarked on one of the major religious cleansing wars that were seen in Arabia and beyond at that time. Although the inquisitions started right after Muhammad's death in 632 AD, they intensified during Abu Bakr, Omar and Uthman, and any one in Arabia and beyond who was suspected of apostasy was killed instantly.

I, the writer of this book, had the heartbreaking chance of visiting a mass grave open to the public of people who resisted Islam during the reigns of the first two caliphs, Abu Bakr and Omar. The grave was located twenty miles south east of the city of Medina. The area extended for about a mile and half to two miles. One Saudi friend, who rejected Islam for what it is, took me there and we dug two feet down in the rubble, pebbles, and sand and I saw human skulls and skeletons. We would move fifty meters to another direction and dig again and then we would find human skulls and skeletons again. Then we would move a hundred meters to another direction and dig and we would also find human skulls and skeletons. There were heaps and mounds of buried bodies over an area of about four square miles. My Saudi companion told me that these were the bodies of what Muslims identify as enemies of Islam, or simply those who refused to convert to Islam or openly resisted Muslims during the times of Abu Bakr, Omar and Uthman. They were the victims of "Riddah Wars." They were also called in Islamic history sources *Murtadin* or apostates if they rejected Islam after they adopted it and discovered it was a false religion. All these atrocities against *Murtadin* are recorded in Islamic sources and Muslims are not ashamed of those atrocities. Muslims actually teach these atrocious incidents with pride and delight to school children and in Islamic festivals as a mark of Islamic triumph over its "enemies." The mass grave itself is a place visited by radicals to pride themselves of their ancestors' courage and strong faith that enabled them to kill that many people in their "holy war" to spread Islam. The mass grave is open to anyone who wants to see a testimony of radical Muslims' shameful past.

The second recorded inquisition and acts of religious cleansing in the history of Islam that Islamic sources and records point out proudly are those during the establishment of the first Saudi state of Muhammad Ibn Saud (b. 1701 -d. 1765 AD) and his religious ally Muhammad Ibn Abdel Wahab (b.1703 - d. 1792 AD). The latter is the one who started Wahabism in the eighteenth century and continues to rule Islamic thought and Islamic theology, jurisprudence, and political ideology until today.

Muhammad Ibn Abdel Wahab launched a campaign of terror against all tribes in Arabia and beyond up to the borders of Syria and Iraq. Wahabists killed all those who did not subscribe to their Wahabi extreme Islam. They plundered all the victims' property in the name of Islam and Allah. Whole towns in Arabia in the eighteenth century were evacuated from its citizens who were tied up and slaughtered; spoils were given to the fighters as they were spoils from Allah which the Quran sanctions.

Following in the footsteps of Abdel Wahab and Wahabism was the Taliban in Afghanistan and Pakistan, Islamic Shabab Movement in Somalia, Boko Haram in Nigeria and West Africa, Gamaat Islamia and Jihad Islami in Algeria, Tunisia, Chechnya, and Mali, the Muslim Brotherhood in Egypt, Syria, Tunis, ISIL in several countries and many other movements that lead a war on anyone who does not follow their extremist brand of Islam whether Christian, Jewish, Hindu, Humanist, moderate Muslim or nonaffiliated. It is noteworthy to mention that Al-Qaeda group is the "basis" of all those violent groups; it is the operative militant wing that mutually inspired and structured all others while the Muslim Brotherhood provides the radical ideology for all.

The Taliban, for example, during their reign in Afghanistan in the eighties and nineties of the twentieth century and even after their fall have claimed hundreds of thousands of people as their victims. This happened during our life time. They changed the way of life not only in Afghanistan but in the whole world. All the terrorist attacks on the West from 1991 to 2010 were planned in Afghanistan and Pakistan by the Taliban and their allies, namely Al-Qaeda, around the globe. The massacres committed by the Taliban have been documented by the United Nations special report.

Boko Haram Islamic Movement in Nigeria and in other countries in western Africa has started a new terror campaign against Christians in Nigeria, and they claimed hundreds of victims in a very short time already. Many Churches have been savagely blown up and burned while Christian worshippers were inside during Sunday services in many Nigerian cities.

***

Countries where Islam is dominant, Islamic inquisitions are in effect; freethinking and the arts are prohibited. A person's religious beliefs are completely censored and policed by the Wahabis-Salafis members of society. This is already in effect in Saudi Arabia, Somalia, Sudan and many other countries. There is no such a thing as freedom of choice or religious freedom. Members of other religions are not allowed to worship in public or speak about their religions.

In Egypt, if a woman, Christian or Muslim, who is not wearing Al-Hijab, the head cover, is more likely than not to be physically assaulted and emotionally abused. In some parts of Egypt, wearing the head cover is not enough; "a good true Muslim woman should even cover her face," the extremists claim. Christian churches have been brutally attacked and burned down in recent years in Egypt; many more Christians were killed.

In Tunis, Algeria, Egypt, Pakistan and Somalia, freethinkers are systematically assassinated; anybody who does not subscribe to the extremists' strict code of Wahabi-Salafi Islam is living in constant fear. A total ban on the arts and non-religious festivals is in effect in Somalia and Sudan.

Muslim extremists everywhere in the world are anti-anything that is not in the Quran; things that are taken for granted such as playing or watching sports, listening to or playing music, clapping, singing, riding bicycles, flying kites (yes, flying kites), drawing, painting, making or owning stuffed animals or dolls, dancing and many other activities have been prohibited by extremists.

***

Muslim extremists use a spate of tactics that help them lick into shape their helpless fellow citizens. They first claim that they are speaking in the name of Allah and that they are mandated by Allah to carry out their acts. That means if someone disobeys the orders of the extremists, then he or she is disobeying Allah right away. Extremists often cite verses from the Quran such as:

"The only religion that Allah accepts is Islam." (Aal-Omran, 19)

And another verse states:

"Fight those who do not believe in Allah, nor in the hereafter, nor do they abide by what Allah and His Messenger have prohibited, nor follow the religion of truth (Islam), out of those who have been given the Book (Jews and Christians), until they pay the tax in acknowledgment of your superiority and they are in a state of humiliation." (Al-Touba, 29)

Extremists also quote a Saying by the prophet Muhammad which incites Muslims to kill non-believers, called "Koffar" or infidels:

"Wherever you find infidels kill them; for whoever kills them shall have reward on the Day of Resurrection."

A verse in Al-Touba says the same:

"And when the respite months have passed, then kill the polytheists (infidels) wherever you see them; and capture them and besiege them and sit in wait for them in ambush." (Al-Touba, 5)

In addition to killing, extremists use torture which is sanctioned by both the Quran and the state; in the Chapter of Al-Touba, for example, several verses authorize Muslims to use torture without check and it is often approved by the state itself as in Egypt, Saudi Arabia, Sudan, Tunis, Iran, and Somalia. Long jail terms are another scare tactic used often to deter would-be freethinkers. Laws that are used are called anti-blasphemy laws which are basically a legal apparatus to destroy any person who would dare to criticize Islam or Muslim leaders.

Muslim extremists have a huge arsenal to oppress men as well as women. Men are considered true Muslims if they grow a sizable beard; the thicker, the better. In countries such as Saudi Arabia, Pakistan, Iran, Somalia, Egypt and many more, men find themselves forced to grow a beard or they do not get jobs and become untrustworthy. Women, on the other hand, are forced to cover their hair and in many places their face or they become the target of all sorts of abuse. Extremists always find verses in the Quran and the prophet's life to enforce their control over people. A society of bearded men and covered women is their ideal Muslim society and that guarantees the extremists' control and power since everyone is in line, obedient and submissive. Extremists are now looking beyond their borders towards the West. They have plans to do the same in Western countries.

Islam is the only religion that denigrates other religions with unchecked freedom. Radical Muslims, in fact, malign the faith and tenets of all others who do not believe in Islam so much so that they punish all others by killing them if they do not believe in Islam since the Quran itself instructs them unequivocally to do so.

Islam does not hold any respect to other religions. There is no freedom of religion in a Muslim society and any apostasy is punishable by death.

The Quran is fraught with verses that incite Muslims to kill anyone who is not following Islam. For example:

"Slay non-believers wherever you find them, and take them, and confine them, and lie in wait for them at every place of ambush." Al-Touba, 5

The same message is repeated in more than 93 different verses in many parts of the Quran such as Al-Nisaa 89, Al-Anfal 39, and Al-Touba 29-30. All these verses directly command Muslims to slaughter Christians, Jews, and all non-believers in Islam.

On the other hand, Islam disparages and derides the beliefs and doctrines of other religions. For example:

"Those (Christians) are infidels who say, 'God is the Third of Three. No god is there but One God." (Al-Maeda, 73)

"Those (Christians) are unbelievers who say, 'God is the Messiah, Mary's son.'" (Al-Maeda, 17)

These verses undeniably and disdainfully vilify Christian beliefs and principles without any respect to Christians' feelings or sentiments. On the other hand, Muslims will never accept any criticism of their religion; instead, they give themselves total freedom to denigrate others' beliefs.

Chapter Nine

The Quran and Its Charm

The question that was nagging many was why Islam succeeded from the start. It did not take me much to find out. The secret is in the magical power of the Quran. For us in the West, we know how powerful the word on our senses and emotions. We know how poetry and music can send us into a trance. The Quran has that power and much more.

Early Muslims admit of that magical thrill as the first element that drew them to the new religion that no one knew about or heard of. At the same time, non-believers of Muhammad or Islam admit of that magical lure of the Quran. They struggled, they admit, to stay away from the irresistible magnetism of the Quran. They describe it as "language of melodious enchantment mixed with awesome effect on the heart, ear, and mind that one can hardly stay away from." Moreover, Muhammad contemporaries who never experienced anything like that and tried to resist Islam and the Quran's charm often accused Muhammad of being "a sorcerer and a supernatural poet who manipulated language for his benefit and managed to capture hearts irredeemably."

The Quran was written in classical Arabic in the first half of the Seventh Century CE, and used the dialect of Mecca, specifically the dialect of the biggest tribe in Mecca, the tribe of Quraish (this is one proof that the Quran is not universal or eternal as Muslims claim but written by a native of Quraish). Historically, the Arabs of that area, and wherever the Arabic language has been used in Arabia, past and present, tend to pride themselves on being good users of classical standard Arabic (the language of the Quran) and of being great poets.

The Quran is Muhammad's miracle. This is what Muhammad and Muslims claim. What does that mean? Moses drowned the Pharaoh and his army after splitting the Red Sea (or the sea of reeds) according to the Old Testament, while Jesus Christ healed the sick, regained eye sight to the blind, and resurrected the dead. Muhammad came up with a miracle of his own so much so that, Muhammad boasts, "No one can match the power of the Quran," even though the tribe of Quraish was the hub of poets and best writers. They could not come up with anything close to the magic of the Quran; hence, this is how gripping the Quran is, and, accordingly, we can understand what it can do to whoever reads or hears it.

The power and magic of the Quran come in three platforms:

1- In its form: music, euphony, rhythm, beat, harmony, synchronization, counterpoint, strident tempo, cadence, lilt, lyricism, pulse, melody, tune, and all formal features of poeticism and music.

2- In its content: ideas expressed through flowery figurative language, tropes such as metaphors, similes, metonymy, synecdoche, hyperbole, irony, etc.

3- In its pragmatics or the intended meaning: that includes statements of pragmatic functions (i.e. Speech Acts, both illocutionary and perlocutionary) that are meant to threaten, browbeat, intimidate, overawe, daunt, give hope, coax, charm, allure, persuade, insult, mock, promise (of rewards or punishment) praise, tease, ridicule, entice, flatter, taunt, scorn, censure, sneer at, caution, warn, reprimand, chastise, exaggerate punishment, maximize rewards, inflate danger, embellish consequences, strike fear (of Allah or Satan), overstate description, overstress urgency, amplify anger, augment satisfaction, etc. All these pragmatic functions are coated profusely in metadiscourse markers, i.e. words and phrases that are hedges, boosters (words that emphasize certainty), attitude markers (words that intimidate or persuade), engagement markers (words that influence), evidentials (giving a possible bad consequence if one does not obey), and self mentions (e.g. naming Allah as the final authority), etc.

The positive pragmatic functions such as praising, flattering, promising, etc. are normally reserved for followers and supporters of Islam and Muhammad. On the other hand, negative pragmatic functions are geared toward beating down those who feel suspicious about Muhammad or critical of his motives and practices, or simply not believing in Muhammad. Therefore, intimidating, exaggerating promised punishment, scorning, ridiculing, browbeating, etc. are exclusively reserved for infidels, doubters, and non-followers of Muhammad.

Before giving some detailed examples, I would like to explain how strident tempo, for instance, is used. It would be coupled with a statement, for example, that signifies a threat. So combining the right form (strident tempo) with the right pragmatic function (threatening) is done to magnify the effect. Similarly, euphony and a melodious structure of words and sounds (form) are usually coupled with a metaphor (content) signifying a generous reward (pragmatics) for the believers and followers of Muhammad and the Islamic faith. On the other hand, a negative, scary form and meaning are brilliantly coupled together for increased effect. By the same token, a positive form and meaning are intertwined together for a stronger effect than if just one alone was used. Therefore, when the three components of the Quran i.e. form, content, and pragmatics are jointly present in a verse (which actually happens in all of the Quran), the power and charm are exponentially increased.

Flowery language is one tool used amply in the Quran. The Quran's content is studded with so many figures of speech that appeal to both the senses and the imagination. In this respect, metaphors, metonymies, and similes, for example, permeate the Quran to lend power to meaning. Therefore, content, joined with form and pragmatics, create a combination of tremendously powerful discourse full of charm and appeal. For instance, the following verse shows the power of figurative language in carrying over meaning, coupled with the two other components, namely, form and pragmatics:

"He entranced you with drowsiness instilling security from Him to you and sent down upon you from the sky rain by which to purify you and remove from you the evil misgivings of Satan and to make steadfast your hearts and plant firmly thereby your feet." (Al-Anfaal, 11)

The verse should be taken entirely on a metaphorical level but it carries both a pragmatic function and poetic charm.

A recurring pragmatic function in the Quran is browbeating doubters and dissenters by promising them great punishment. For example:

"Allah sealed their hearts and hearing, and placed over their vision a veil. And for them is a great punishment." (Al-Baqara, 7)

One notices in this verse the use of an extended figure of speech where a metaphor is coupled with a metonymy. There are numerous instances of intimidation similar to the one above such as:

"And fear Allah and know that Allah's penalty is severe." (Al-Baqara, 196)

Another example is:

"And as for those who disbelieved, I will punish them with a severe punishment in this world and the Hereafter, and they will have no helpers." (Aal-Omran, 56)

Thus, the verses plainly intend to browbeat those who merely doubt or disbelieve in Allah or Muhammad. There are as many as ninety-eight verses promising burning in hell for eternity and other types of punishment for anyone dissenting with Muhammad or Allah.

Another pragmatic function often employed in the Quran is insulting non-followers and non-believers of Muhammad and Allah by portraying them as sick, foolish, and handicapped or as just mere liars as in:

"In their hearts is disease, so Allah has increased their disease; and for them there is a painful punishment because they [habitually] used to lie." (Al-Baqara, 10)

The same message is delivered in another verse:

"Unquestionably, it is they who are the foolish, but they know [it] not." (Al-Baqara, 13)

The promise of depression, destitution, and blindness for non-believers is delivered in the following verse:

"And whoever turns away from My Quran - indeed, he will have a depressed, impoverished life, and We will shove him on the Day of Resurrection all blind." (Taha, 124)

Verses of this import permeate the Quran with the intent to insult and intimidate those who simply do not believe in Allah, the Quran, or Muhammad. The number of these verses totals seventy-six.

Similarly, taunting, trivializing, shaming, belittling, and mocking any person who is not submitting to Muhammad's religion is common in the Quran. For example,

"Whoever turns away from the Quran - then indeed, he will come on the Day of Resurrection carrying a burden, living eternally in their burden, and evil it is for them on the Day of Resurrection as a load. The Day the Horn will be blown. And We will gather the criminals that Day, blue-eyed. They will murmur among themselves: You remained not but ten days in the world. We are most knowing of what they say when the best of them in turn will say: You remained not but one day in the world." (Taha, 100-104)

These verses mock those who do not believe as they will turn up on the Day of Judgment carrying a load of sins because they did not believe in the Quran and then they are called "criminals" for that and then they taunt each other of how long they could survive in the world without the belief in the Quran (ten days, one day).

Verses of that type are intended to brainwash and condition people to the fact that Allah and the Quran are a must and if one should miss them, then one is in eternal torment and damnation. The Quran is full of those verses. Such verses preclude any reasonable attempt by people to question the Quran, its content or authenticity. There are many verses that state plainly that questioning Allah or Muhammad is a horrendous sin punishable by eternity in hell.

This kind of brainwashing and mind control is a linguistic pragmatic tactic often used in the Quran. There are many of those sweet-sour verses of juxtaposition where believers are promised the best of rewards while non-believers are assured punishment and annihilation. An example of as many as seventy-seven of such occurrences is:

"And that who obeys Allah and His Messenger (Muhammad) - God will admit him to Gardens beneath which rivers flow; but that who turns away - God will penalize him with painful punishment. Unquestionably, Allah was content with the believers when they pledged allegiance to you, [O Muhammad], under the tree, and He knew what was in their hearts, so He sent down tranquility upon them and rewarded them with an immediate conquest (over non-believers)." (Al-Fatah, 17-18)

The tactic speaks for itself. If you come along, Allah will reward you. If you do not, you will be severely punished and lose your battle. The power of suggestion. This kind of allure-intimidation juxtaposition, of mental manipulation works easily on most people who are seeking help. Effectively, it is an excellent psychological skill that Muhammad was cognizant of and he knew how to use it very adroitly in building a throng of followers. Assuming power and claiming that Allah can do all those feats was a very shrewd method of deliberate choice by Muhammad.

Exaggerating Allah's supreme power and His ability to inflict ordeals on those who do not comply with his will is pervading the Quran. It is a ready technique to mind-control and brainwash people while scaring non-believers. One example of so many in the Quran is:

> *"And the thunder exalts Allah, praise to Him - and the angels as well, out of fear of Him - and Allah sends thunderbolts and strikes therewith whom He desires if they (non-believers) question Him; and He is severe in His punishment."* (Al-Raad, 13)

Rewards for the believers comprise lots of materialistic pleasures in the promised paradise such as fruits, rivers of honey, meats, virgins, gold, and servants. For non-believers, fire for eternity and horrendous torture are in store for them. An instance of this is in the following verse:

> *"Of Paradise, which the righteous are promised, wherein are rivers of water unaltered, rivers of milk the taste of which never changes, rivers of wine delicious to those who drink, and rivers of purified honey, in which they will have all fruits and forgiveness from their Lord, but there are those who abide eternally in the Fire and are given to drink scalding water that will grind their intestines."* (Muhammad, 15)

A similar verse in which lavish materialistic life is promised states that:

> *"They (the believers) will have gardens as perpetual abode; beneath them rivers will flow. They will be adorned therein*

with bracelets of gold and will wear green garments of fine silk and brocade, reclining therein on adorned couches. Excellent is the reward, and comfortable is the resting place." (Al-Kahf, 31)

Sexual indulgence is unashamedly promised. This pragmatic function of alluring and amplifying rewards for believers in Muhammad and Allah is stated in more than one hundred and seventy-eight verses. Men are assured in Muhammad's paradise of women for sex and boys to serve them. Here is one example:

"They (the believers) will be reclining on thrones lined up, and We will pair them off with fair women with large, [beautiful] eyes. ....And We will provide them with fruit and meat of whatever they crave. They will exchange with one another a cup [of wine] wherein there will be no idle conversation or act of sin. There will be boys going around for them, as if they were pearls studded in." (Al-Tour, 20-24).

In other verses where a very sinister promise of paradise and pleasure is conditional not just on following Muhammad and the Quran but upon killing in the name of Allah and Muhammad all non-believers. There are eight verses that unequivocally state that. An example is:

"Indeed, Allah has purchased from the believers their lives and their properties in exchange for that they will have Paradise. They fight in the cause of Allah, so they kill and be killed. This is a true promise binding upon Him...." (Al-Touba, 111)

Perhaps the strongest pragmatic function of all that gave Muhammad and the Quran the protection needed from any accusation of making up a new false religion and claiming false prophecy is the pre-emptive self-immunization pragmatic function. This is also called *prolepsis*; it is a rhetorical pragmatic technique where the writer or speaker anticipates possible objection or doubt and thus answering them in advance and dispelling any doubt by spelling out such objections and doubts as unfounded. The psychological effect is stunning and utterly mesmerizing since the recipient is left with nothing to do or say.

This practically means that Muhammad expected criticism from Mecca's residents for his Quran and his claim of being a prophet; so in anticipation, the Quran came with verses such as the following verses to preclude any future condemnation of the Quran for being forged or of Muhammad for being a false prophet.

"This is the Book about which there is no doubt." (Al-Baqara, 2)

Similarly, another verse preemptively states the same proposition:

"Certainly, it is We (Allah) who revealed the Qur'an and indeed, We will be its protector." (Al-Hajar, 9)

Even further, the following verse seems to clench the argument for Muhammad and the Quran:

"Certainly, this is a noble Quran; in a book well-protected; none would touch it unless they are pure." (Al-Waqiaa, 77-79)

There were many claims and accusations that Muhammad was mad and hallucinating at the time he came up with his religion, so to shoot down these claims preemptively, the Quran states by way of prolepsis:

"And your fellow is not [at all] mad." (Al-Takweer, 22)

And further, the Quran mocks the residents of Mecca and divulging their fears and concerns which they expressed during one of their private meetings to discuss Muhammad's claims of prophecy:

"And they (Mecca residents) were saying, "Are we to leave our gods for a mad poet?"" (Al-Safaat, 36)

This tactic of the Quran was a very effective tool used to preempt and obstruct any potential condemnation of Muhammad or the Quran during his time and for centuries down the road. It was a very resourceful tactic that apparently worked well and efficiently. There are about twenty-seven verses of this purport peppered all over the Quran.

The Quran was interestingly "revealed" piecemeal. In other words, it was written bit by bit, i.e. a verse or a group of verses at a time, to accommodate for the current events that were going on in Mecca, to defend Muhammad and justify his actions at certain times, and to get around any objections or doubts raised against Muhammad or the Quran. The Quran was also used opportunely in many occasions. An example of how the Quran was a tool of convenience for Muhammad is when he wanted to marry the wife of his adopted son, Zayd Ibn Harithah. Islamic sources mention that Muhammad saw her face and liked the beautiful wife of Zayd. In the Arabia society, it was taboo for a father to marry his daughter in-law even after divorce, so what does the Quran do? A verse was "revealed" readily clearing the way for Muhammad to mate with his adopted son's wife as a command from Allah to marry her. That shows how the Quran was a tool of justification to enhance Muhammad's status and show that he is a prophet allowed to do what others cannot do while keeping the holy image of a respected prophet who acts upon the commands of Allah. The verse is:

"And [remember, O Muhammad], when you said to the one on whom Allah bestowed favor and you bestowed favor on him (your adopted son), "Keep your wife and fear Allah," while you concealed within yourself that which Allah is to disclose. And you feared the people (of Mecca), while Allah has more right that you fear Him. So when Zayd had no longer any need for her, We married her to you in order that there not be upon the believers any concern regarding the wives of their adopted sons when they no longer have need of them. And ever is Allah's command to be fulfilled." (Al-Ahzab, 37)

Another unethical and unscrupulous pragmatic function used in the Quran is defaming, insulting and sneering at individuals who simply did not (or do not since the present tense is often used in those verses) accept Muhammad as a prophet. The Quran's tactic is to make an example of someone or a group of individuals, so others would be apprehensive and greatly frightened to show the least opposition to Muhammad or Islam. An example is in:

"May the hands of Abu Lahab be ruined and ruined is he. His wealth will not avail him or that which he gained. He will go to hell and burn in a blazing flame. And his woman as well - the carrier of firewood. Around her neck is a rope of palm tree dried leaves." (Al-Masad, 1-5)

This chapter of the Quran, titled Al-Masad, is part of a smear campaign launched against a true gentleman from Mecca named Abd Al-Uzza (died 624 AD) and his kind decent wife Arwa, also named Umm Jamil (died 629 AD). They were loving, well-off people who only refused to support Muhammad. They were very stylish and elegant. In the verses above, they are referred to as " Abu Lahab [Father Fire] and his Woman." Abd Al-Uzza liked music and helped the poor of Mecca. Sadly, Muhammad and his followers called him names such as infidel, non-believer, and Abu Lahab (Father Fire). The truth was that he was very educated by the standards of his time and so was his wife, Arwa. They were very polite and courteous. The prophet Muhammad felt they were taking the wind out of his sails, so he began his campaign of defamation against the couple.

The Quran states that Abd Al-Uzza's hand would be ruined and that he would find no help in his money or possessions and that his wife referred to as the" woman" or the "broad," a demeaning word for a lady of her status, is carrying firewood and has a rope around her neck made of palm tree dried leaves, a disparaging image of this lady. The portrayal is just enough proof of the amount of hatred Muhammad and the Quran had harbored against the couple for not believing in him.

It is my duty as a writer and historian to do the couple some justice after that horrendous portrayal for so many centuries for no crime other than disbelieving in Muhammad. For more than fourteen centuries, they have been jeered at and related in stories to children around the Muslim world as a wicked, evil couple. The truth of the matter is that they were not. They committed no crime. They were like the millions of us today who are attacked in the name of Allah because we have another religion or belief. The Quran is fraught with such portrayal of totally innocent people, but that was one of the pragmatic tactical functions used to stem any similar attempt by anyone to oppose the prophet Muhammad, in the past or even at the present time. In Islamic later writings, stories of how ugly looking the couple appeared, even though they were a very handsome couple, were made. Furthermore, they were rumored that they died of a very contagious repulsive skin disease, but all these stories were a continuation of the legacy started in the Quran.

On the other hand, the Quran used music and poeticism massively. To illustrate the poetic and rhythmic charm of the Quran, the following is a transliterated Chapter (Al-Shams, 1-10) from the Quran where one feels the lilt and cadence very clearly which, even if the reader does not speak Arabic, will likely feel:

"Wal shamsu Wa dohaha,

Wal qamaru iza talaha,

Wal naharu iza galaha,

Wal leilu iza gashaha,

Wa sama'u wa banaha,

Wal ardu wama tahaha,

Wal nafsu wama sawaha

Fa al hama ha

Fugu ruha wa taqwaha,

Qad af laha mann zak kaha,

Wa qad haba mann das saha."

The combination of the internal vowels and the rhyme scheme has an immense effect on the listener. In addition, there is a very subtle play on the internal beat of the verses that creates a mystic sensation.

Another part of many in the Quran where lilt and poeticism are felt strong are the following verses from Al-Ghashiya, 4-12:

"Tasla naran hamiya tan,

Tusqa min ayenin aniya tin,

Laiysa laham ta aam

Il la min daree,

La yusmin wa la yugnee

Min guu in,

Wu guhun yauma izin

Na ima tun,

Li saa iyha

Ra diya tun,

Fi gan natin

Aa liya tin,

La tas ma uu fiyha

La giyatan,

Aiy nun gariya tun."

In the above verses, the use of the recurrent short phrases and short vowels has a strong impression on the listener and leaves a beating lilt for a long while after listening to the verses. Music is masterfully interwoven with a mesh of figures of speech in these verses.

It is significant at this point to state that there are some verses from other scriptures such as the Old Testament of similar content to the Quranic pragmatic functions. It is crucial to emphasize that the Quranic statements are speech acts directly addressed to people with the intention to carry out certain pragmatic functions unlike other books such as the Talmud or the Old Testament where mentioning God's anger and fury as just reminders and they do not mean to intimidate or browbeat, which is the signature of the Quran's way of stating pragmatic functions. Pragmatic functions in the Quran have the psychological impact that arrests the mind and numbs sensible reasoning, leaving the reader or listener no chance to think logically and thus surrender to what is being said, and that is one secret of the immense power of the Quran.

On the whole, that rhetorical accomplishment of the Quran is the secret for its effect on both listeners and readers alike. On the other hand, reciting it which has become an art and a profession in itself by professional reciters and readers amplify the three components mentioned above. One professional reader or reciter of the Quran told me that "A recitation of the Quran is eurhythmic and that is all it needs to enchant and grip the emotions of a listener no matter who."

Another issue that is worthy of pointing out is that Muslims do not accept translating the Quran. They claim, which is a right claim, that much of the meaning and effect will be lost in translation. That is absolutely true because, not only the music, poeticism, figurative meaning, and the pragmatics of discourse will be lost but also the added total effect of all of these components will be impaired or mangled up and may give a counter effect. In other words, the total aesthetic magnetism of the original Arabic text will lose much or all of its purpose. However, meaning remains intact to a large extent and meaning alone has fascinated millions of people who never spoke Arabic and got enchanted by the pragmatic import of the verses after translation to many languages.

The Quran itself boasts that no one can ever emulate its style or its miraculous content. Despite the fact that the Quran is a linguistic feat and a poetic miracle, by admission of Islamic scholars and sources, yet, there is a structural flaw and a thematic fault in it. To be more specific, most Quran verses do not hold together thematically; there is no cohesion or coherence. Each Chapter of the Quran has a multitude of disconnected ideas and themes that do not relate to one another; sometimes the incongruity is inside the same verse. For example:

"And if you fear that you will not deal justly with orphans, then marry those that please you of women, two or three or four. But if you fear that you will not be just, then marry one only or those your right hand possesses. That is more convenient that you may not tend to injustice." (Al-Nisaa, 3)

The above verse starts with talk about the possibility of doing injustice to orphans; then, it suddenly shifts to licensing men to commit polygamy or to have concubines. The verse is completely incoherent like many parts of the Quran. The Arabic text sounds even more incoherent than the English translation, but some Muslim radicals try to justify the lack of coherence and the absence of cohesion by saying that the verse meant that marrying mothers of orphans will do justice for both (the mothers and the orphans). The verse does not say that meaning at all.

Although the Quran boasts precision of facts and perfection of thoroughness, contradictions and inconsistencies abound in the Quran. For example, in one verse, the Quran states Allah created earth and heaven in eight days:

> *"Say, "Do you indeed disbelieve in He who created the earth in two days and believe in equals to Him? He is the Lord of the whole universe ".And He placed on the earth firmly set mountains over its surface, and He blessed it and determined therein its [creatures'] sustenance in four days without distinction - for [the information] of those who ask. Then He directed Himself to the sky while it was smoke and said to it and to the earth, "Come [into being], willingly or by compulsion." They said, "We have come willingly." And He completed the seven skies in two days and inspired in each sky its law."* (Fussilat, 9-12)

However, in three other verses in three different Chapters, the Quran says that Allah created earth and heaven in six days:

> *"Indeed, your Lord is Allah, who created the skies and earth in six days."* (Al-Aaraaf, 54)

The contradiction is not only in the number of days but in the order: earth created first or heavens created first. This inconsistency occurs in many verses such as Al-Nazeaat, 27-32 and Al-Baqara, 29.

Another obvious error is in the following verses where the Quran says that Allah made night and day in the sky.

"He raised the sky's ceiling and proportioned it. And He darkened its night and brought about its morning light." (Al-Nazeaat, 28-29)

Facts are that night and day are phenomena on earth, not in the sky, due to the rotation of the earth around the sun. Night and day are not sky occurrences.

Also, the Quran has many contradictory statements such as:

"And had your Lord willed, those on earth would have believed - all of them entirely. Then, [O Muhammad], would you compel the people so that they become believers?" (Yunis, 99)

This is diametrically opposite to:

"Fight those who do not believe in Allah...." (Al-Touba, 29)

There are other nine similar contradictory occurrences about the same idea in the Quran.

Moreover, the Quran says that Noah and all his family were saved in the Flood:

"And Noah, when he called [to Allah], so We responded to him and saved him and his family from the great flood." (Al-Anbiaa, 76)

But in another Chapter, the Quran says that his son drowned!

"...And Noah called to his son who was apart [from them], "O my son, come aboard with us and be not with the disbelievers. But he said, "I will take refuge on a mountain

to protect me from the water." [Noah] said, "There is no protector today from the decree of Allah, except for whom He gives mercy. And the waves came between them, and he was among the drowned." (Huud, 42-43)

Another striking inconsistency is found in Chapters Al-Aaraf, 107 and Al-Shoaraa, 32 where Moses stick or staff turns into an actual snake:

"So [Moses] threw his staff, and suddenly it was a manifest serpent." (Al-Shoaraa, 32 and Al-Aaraf, 107)

In both verses, the staff unequivocally becomes a snake. However, this contradicts Chapters Al-Naml, 10 and Al-Qasas, 31:

"And [he was told], "Throw down your staff," and he saw it shaking as if it were a snake." (Al-Naml 10)

In this verse, the staff did not turn into a snake but it shook "*as if*" it were a snake. It is a big difference and a gigantic contradiction between "a manifest snake" in one verse and "shaking as if it were a snake" in another.

Another blatant inconsistency is found in the fate of the Pharaoh who chased Moses and the Israelites:

"...and indeed I think, O Pharaoh, that you are destroyed. So he intended to drive them from the land, but We drowned him and those with him all together." (AL-Israa, 102-103)

This is emphasized again in Al-Zokhrof, 55 where the Pharaoh was definitely "drowned" and "destroyed." However, this is not the meaning in Yunis, 92 where the Pharaoh was actually saved in body:

"So today We will save you in body that you may be to those who succeed you a sign. And indeed, many among the people, of Our signs, are heedless." (Yunis, 92)

Another blatant contradiction is found in:

"But We threw him [Yunis] onto the open shore while he was ill." (Al-Safaat, 145)

Here the prophet Yunis was thrown onto the open which is not the same as:

"If without that favor from his Lord made to him (Yunis), he would have been thrown onto the open shore while he was reprimanded." (Al-Qalam, 49)

In Aal-Omran, 67, "Ibraham was……a Muslim." And in Yunis, 72, Noah "was ordered to be of the Muslims."

This comes in negation to Muhammad's confirmation in Al-Anaam, 163, "I am the first Muslim."

Another error is found in Chapter Yaseen, 38.

"And the sun runs [on course] toward its settling point."

The verse states that after night falls on earth, the sun settles down during night time according to both Ibn Katheer and Al-Qurtobi exegeses. This is a serious lapse in the Quran as well. The sun rotates on its axis. The sun moves in its orbit around the barycenter of the solar system. The sun also revolves around the center of our Galaxy all the time. The sun never stops or settles. It actually gives light in another part of the world.

So far, this section showed the tip of the iceberg of barefaced contradictions and errors in the Quran. There are more than a hundred other discrepancies and inaccuracies that need a separate book to catalogue; they are all errors that are contrary to facts, linguistic mistakes, and contextual contradictions. The above mentioned contradictions, though, explain why Islam prohibits scrutinizing or criticizing the Quran. Radicals do not want anyone to expose Islam's weaknesses.

The Quran was "revealed" piecemeal over so many years. In addition, the collection of the Quran took place years after Muhammad's death, and the death of the prophet's companions who memorized it; also, the collection itself was a primitive and a shoddy process. Finally, there were many interpolations and changes that were done in the Quran as it will be shown later in Chapter 12 of this book.

However, several non-Arabic speakers admit falling under the spell of listening to recited Quran in Arabic and its noticeable music, which is just one component of the Quran. It is like listening to Italian opera singers and be gripped by its artistic beauty and aesthetic splendor without knowing a word in the Italian language. Just one would think of Pavarotti or the three tenors singing. Nevertheless, not all people fall to that reciting magic of the Quran, yet that shows what a powerful delight and charm the Quran can produce.

Chapter Ten

An Empirical Study of the Quran's Charm and Power

To calibrate and assess methodically and analytically the extent of the Quran's linguistic and musical charm and power on both Muslims and non-Muslims, a survey was conducted. There were 438 subjects in this study. They were selected randomly from four countries, namely, Saudi Arabia, Egypt, Britain, and the United States. The subjects of the study were from a diverse population, namely, different nationalities, education levels, age bands, gender, religions, linguistic backgrounds, social and economic classes, and ethnicities.

The project had two parts:

1- **A Questionnaire**: A detailed questionnaire that was conducted to gauge the Quran's charm on the subjects of the survey. The respondents of this group were all Muslims who were both native speakers of Arabic and non-native speakers of Arabic.

The questionnaire involved twenty-five questions such as "Do you read the Quran regularly?", "Do you listen to recitations of the Quran?" Regarding the most effective parts of the Quran, there were questions such as "Which aspect or aspects of the Quran are more powerful and charming? e.g., its music, lyricism, and poeticism, its figurative language, its promise of paradise, and which promise is the most enticing such as food, virgins, rivers." Other questions were about what is more effective: the form or the content of the Quran, if the Quran's poeticism and music are the major reasons to love the Quran, if the Quran's promises of rewards in paradise are a major reason to love the Quran, and whether they prefer to read or listen to the Quran more. There were also questions about the Quran's pragmatic functions such as threats of punishment, sneering, intimidation, etc. There were also questions about whether they "believe everything in the Quran, how rational and consequential is the Quran, and whether the Quran is Allah's word." The subjects were to choose from a two-point scale of "Not at all" and "Certainly yes."

2- **An Experiment:** The second part of the survey was an experiment involving subjects who had never been exposed to the Quran before or never believed in it even though they were partially exposed to it as they were Christian speakers of Arabic living in Egypt. In other words, the experiment was conducted on exclusively non-Muslims to measure the effect of the Quran on them. They were given passages to read and also listened as part of the experiment to three portions of the Quran. It is noteworthy to mention again that the subjects in this experiment were non-Muslim, both native speakers of Arabic and non-native speakers of Arabic and lived all their lives in Egypt (Christians), The United States of America, and Britain.

There were two parts in this experiment:

- First part (Reading): The non-native speakers of Arabic subjects from the United States of America and Britain were given written translated portions of the Quran that involved different themes and topics ranging from threats, torture, promise of paradise, etc. The native speakers of Arabic were given passages in Arabic since they were born and raised in Egypt even though they were Christian.

- Second part (Listening): All the subjects of this group (both the native and the non-native speakers of Arabic) listened to three portions of recited Quran in Arabic (each portion was about five minutes long) by professional well-known readers (reciters) famous for their melodious voices, namely, Muhammad Rifaat and Taha Al-Fashni.

Then the subjects of this non-Muslim group were given a questionnaire and were asked twenty questions about whether they felt moved by the Quran's music, lyricism, lilt, cadence, the reader's voice. For the written translated portions, the subjects were asked if they felt threatened by the torture, if they did not believe in the Quran as the word of Allah, if they would consider converting to Islam, If they would listen to the Quran again on their own, If they found the Quran convincing, if they felt enticed by the promise of paradise and the potential of having virgins and food, if the Quran sounded like the word of God, if they felt the Quran was the word of man, etc. The subjects were also to choose from a two-point scale of "Not at all" and "Certainly yes."

The 438 subjects of the study were of two main groups:

1- Muslims (a total of 346 native speakers of Arabic and non-native speakers of Arabic). This is the group that took only the first part of the study, i.e., the Questionnaire.

2- Non-Muslims (they were 92 of native and non-native speakers of Arabic). This is the group that took only the second part of the study, i.e., the Experiment.

The first group consisted of 346 respondents to the questionnaire. This group included:

I- 201 Muslim native speakers of Arabic. They were born in Arabic speaking countries and they were Saudis, Egyptians, Syrians, Yemenis, and Jordanians working in Saudi Arabia. The subjects of this group were interviewed in 2010 and 2011 in Saudi Arabia.

II- 145 Muslim non-native speakers of Arabic. They were mainly Indians, Bangladeshis, Philippines, Turks, and Pakistanis who lived and worked in Saudi Arabia. 96 of them were born Muslims but never learned Arabic as a first language. They only memorize parts of the Quran in Arabic. 49 were converts to Islam. The subjects of this group were interviewed in 2010 and 2011. They were interviewed in Saudi Arabia.

In the Non-Muslim group, there were 92 subjects. The group included:

I- 31 native speakers of Arabic. They were all Christian Egyptians of The Coptic and Catholic faith. They lived all their lives in Egypt and were often exposed to the Quran through Egyptian media and everyday activities. They were interviewed in 2011 and 2012 in Egypt.

II- 61 non-native speakers of Arabic. They were all non-Muslim Americans and English citizens interviewed in their respective countries in 2011 and 2012.

The results of the study show significant facts and indications about the charm and lure of the Quran and its linguistic power, form, and content:

1- 96% of Muslim native speakers of Arabic admit that the Quran's music and poeticism are major reasons for the Quran's greatness and charm.

2- 96% of Muslim native speakers of Arabic admit that the Quran's music and poeticism are major reasons to love and be strongly attracted to the Quran.

3- 94% of Muslim native speakers of Arabic admit that the promise of paradise and its materialistic rewards is a major reason to love the Quran.

4- 92% of Muslim native speakers of Arabic admit that they like to listen more to the Quran than reading it for the lilt and the melody of the recitation.

5- 94% of Muslim native speakers of Arabic admit that the promise of punishment and burning in hell is certain and is a reason to believe in the Quran.

6- 4% of Muslim native speakers of Arabic admit the Quran is not the word of God.

7- 6% of Muslim native speakers of Arabic admit not believing everything in the Quran.

8- 6% of Muslim native speakers of Arabic admit that the Quran sounds irrational and inconsequential in many of its parts.

9- 94% of Muslim native speakers of Arabic admit that the Quran's promise of rewards from Allah in life and in the hereafter is a reason for their belief in Islam.

10- 94% of Muslim native speakers of Arabic admit the mere fear of Allah as portrayed as a fearful God in the Quran is a reason for belief in Islam.

11- 94% of Muslim native speakers of Arabic admit that the lilt and lyricism of the Quran have more power than its content.

12- 94% of Muslim native speakers of Arabic admit that the combination of sound and music, content, and pragmatics is very powerful and effective in attracting them to the Quran and Islam.

As for Muslim non-native speakers of Arabic, the following are among the most significant results of the questionnaire:

13- 98% of Muslim non-native speakers of Arabic admit that the Quran's music and poeticism have a great lure and charm. This is slightly higher than the native speakers' response. It seems here that the Quran's music is even more effective on non-native speakers of Arabic Muslims.

14- 98% of Muslim non-native speakers of Arabic admit that the Quran's music and poeticism are major reasons for the Quran's great lure and charm and their attraction to Islam. This is also slightly higher than the responses of the native speakers of Arabic.

15- 94% of Muslim non-native speakers of Arabic admit that the promise of paradise and its materialistic rewards is a major reason to love the Quran. This is equal to native speakers of Arabic responses.

16- 98% of Muslim non-native speakers of Arabic admit that they like to listen more to the Quran than reading it for the lilt and the melody of the recitation. This is significantly higher than native speakers of Arabic responses.

17- 92% of Muslim non-native speakers of Arabic admit that the Quran's promise of punishment and burning in hell is certain and is a reason to believe in the Quran. This is slightly lower than native speakers of Arabic responses.

18- 6% of Muslim non-native speakers of Arabic admit the Quran is not the word of God. This is slightly higher than native speakers of Arabic responses. This is because Muslim non-native speakers of Arabic are attracted more by the music and poetic charm rather than rational content which they find lacking.

19- 8% of Muslim non-native speakers of Arabic admit not believing everything in the Quran. This is slightly higher than native speakers of Arabic responses. This proves further the effect of the music rather than content or pragmatics.

20- 8% of Muslim non-native speakers of Arabic admit that the Quran sounds irrational and inconsequential in many of its parts. This is slightly higher than native speakers of Arabic responses. Again, this shows the power of Quran's music that attracts rather than rational content or pragmatics.

21- 92% of Muslim non-native speakers of Arabic admit that the promise of rewards from Allah in life and in the hereafter is a reason for their belief in Islam. This is slightly lower than native speakers of Arabic responses.

22- 92% of Muslim non-native speakers of Arabic admit the mere fear of Allah as portrayed as a fearful God in the Quran is a certain reason for belief in Islam. This is slightly lower than native speakers of Arabic responses

23- 98% of Muslim non-native speakers admit that the lilt and lyricism of the Quran have more power than its content.

This is considerably higher than native speakers of Arabic responses.

24- 100% of Muslim converts (they were all non-native speakers of Arabic) admit that the Quran's music and lilt is the major factor of their conversion to Islam.

25- 98% of Muslim non-native speakers of Arabic admit that the combination of sound and music, content, and pragmatics is very powerful and effective in attracting them to the Quran and Islam. This is relatively higher than Muslim native speakers of Arabic responses.

That may help conclude that the Quran's form, i.e. its music and lilt, plays a very crucial role in luring people to Islam. That also explains that among the 1.4 Billion Muslims around the world, there are 1.1 Billion Muslims who do not speak or use Arabic as their first language. It is rather the lilt and music that have the entire lure to Islam and its book, the Quran. Both content and the pragmatics follow in their power and effect on them. However, there is evidence in the data that the combination of form (e.g. music and sound), content (e.g. metaphors), and pragmatics (e.g. the commands and promises) has a collective power and charm in attracting people to the Quran and Islam.

As for the non-Muslims:

26- 12% of non-Muslims admit that the Quran has charm and allure stemming from its music and lilt, while content and pragmatics come after.

27- 94% of non-Muslims admit that they will never consider converting to Islam if they find the Quran alluring and charming.

28- 6% of non-Muslims admit that they find the Quran charming and alluring.

29- 8% of non-Muslims admit that they will read or listen to the Quran on their own.

30- 96% of non-Muslims admit that the threats of the Quran will never move them to believe in the Quran or Islam.

31- 96% of non-Muslims admit that the Quran's promise of rewards of material pleasures will never move them to believe in the Quran or Islam.

32- 96% of non-Muslims admit that the Quran's description of torture is repulsive.

33- 96% of non-Muslims admit that the Quran was not the word of God.

34- 96% of non-Muslims admit that the Quran is irrational and inconsequential.

35- 6% of non-Muslims admit that the Quran's poeticism and musical charm can be the main reason for their conversion rather than its content or pragmatics.

The study reveals the respondents' significant tendencies regarding the lure and magic of the Quran. As the results indicate, there is a significant role played by the form, content, and pragmatic functions of the Quran on the Muslim group. The results also indicate that the Quran's music and poeticism (i.e., its form) are certain reasons for its charm and power. The findings also indicate that the Quran is a major reason, if not the only reason, that attracts people to Islam.

It is also significant that there are Muslims who have raised palpable doubts about the Quran and its authenticity. On the other hand, the study also shows that non-Muslims are far more unlikely to be charmed or affected by the Quran. However, a significant percentage (6%) admits that there is charm in the Quran. Non-Muslims significantly find the Quran far from being the word of God and they do not feel intimidated or lured by the language of the Quran in comparison to Muslims. Albeit, there is a significant percentage of respondents in the non-Muslim group (ranging between 6% to 12% on different items of the questionnaire) that find the Quran alluring and has musical charm.

To conclude, peaceful Muslims find in the Quran a message of serenity and love. As for radicals and extremists, there is no doubt that the magic, power, and charm of the Quran numb their senses; it paralyzes their sound reasoning; it impairs their natural logic; it hampers normal functioning of the brain. No wonder one would see terrorists and radicals in Pakistan, Yemen, Egypt, Libya, Chechnya, Somalia, Sudan, Tunis, Indonesia, etc. and even in Western countries as well, conspiring, plotting, scheming, conniving, planning, raving, raging, rambling, running amok, crazed, frenzied, gibbering, hallucinating, frantic, hysterical, delirious, demented, possessed, manic, and completely out of control as the whole world saw them on numerous occasions for the slightest matters. In a nutshell, radicals use the Quran unreasonably. These radicals are literally and factually under the distorted spell of the Quran. They are bigoted and violent. On the other hand, moderate peaceful Muslims who are the sweeping majority of Muslims enjoy the beauty of the Quran and find peace in it.

Chapter Eleven

Waraqah Ibn Naufal

According to Islamic scholars and documents, Waraqah Ibn Naufal was a Christian Ebionites priest (according to *Sahih Al-Bukhari*, 1/3). He was the Bishop of Mecca. It is very crucial here to point out the relevance of the Ebionites (*Hanif* in Arabic) to the whole story of Islam. Ebionites are a Jewish Christian sect that appeared around 70 AD and were mainly a group of Jews who accepted Jesus as the Messiah but rejected any divine qualities attached to him. The Ebionites followed the Torah and the Gospel of Matthew only. Some scholars and church historians regard the Ebionites as a group of *Judaized* Christians. In other words, for the Ebionites, exactly like Muslims, Jesus is the Messiah but not the Son of God. Nevertheless, they followed the Law of Moses (many of those commandments had been incorporated as principal doctrines of Islam). To be more specific, the Ebionites are defined as a sect stressing the oneness of God and the humanity of Jesus, exactly like Islam. Therefore, the Ebionites were regarded by both the majority of conventional Jews and mainstream gentile Christians as a heretical sect.

Consequently, Ebionite Waraqah Ibn Naufal decided to shed off the negative image and the rejection of the Ebionites sect by crafting a new religion that would encompass Judaism and Christianity and accommodate for every one if possible. No wonder then that Islam appears in many ways entirely Jewish: The Law of Moses is observed, idolatry and gambling are prohibited, no pork, women should cover their hair, male circumcision is emphasized, dietary and health practices of the Jews must be followed, the Jewish greeting Shalom Aleichem (Assalamu Alikum in Arabic) is used in Islam, only the right hand must be used, and placing much emphasis on rituals such as ablution and fasting, etc. (just to name a few shared practices in both Judaism and Islam). Equally, the similarity between Islam and Christianity is immense; Islam reveres Mary and Jesus and accepts Christianity as a religion and Jesus as the Messiah and as a Prophet; moreover, the Gospel of Matthew (which was exclusively followed by the Ebionites) and many of its themes and ideas had been selectively incorporated into the Quran. Many of the early short verses that were "revealed" or rather written by Waraqah Ibn Naufal in Mecca bear a striking similarity to the spirit of the Gospel of Matthew. On the other hand, both Judaism and Christianity revere Jerusalem (exactly as Islam does), and in that way, Waraqah Ibn Naufal wanted a mega religion that would embrace and take in everybody (pun intended; all meanings of "take in" are intended, specifically "to admit", "to include" and "to deceive"). He wanted to unite the two major religions - Judaism and Christianity - into one under a new banner and a new name. Basically, he wanted the Ebionites' beliefs and doctrines to become "Islam." Unsurprisingly, things did not work out the way he planned. So what was Waraqah Ibn Naufal's original plan? And how he proceeded to implement it?

First, Waraqah Ibn Naufal wanted a peaceful world of united religions and sects. This did not fructify. Instead, the world ended up with more conflict and misery. Secondly, he wanted to eliminate both traditional Judaism and mainstream Christianity. Apparently, this did not work out either. Third, he wanted Islam to be the religion that replaces the Ebionites sect in name but survives in doctrine. Muslims are actually observing all Ebionites beliefs under the name of Islam. In his book, *Al-Haratiqah* or *The Heretics* (pages 22 through 79), Uhanna Al-Dimashqui, also known as John of Damascus, (Died 749 AD) affirms Ibn Naufal's Ebionites background and his major role in writing the Quran. Similarly, Saad Bin Mansour Bin Kammounah (Died 1285 AD) affirms Ibn Naufal's role in crafting Islam as well as the falsity of both the Quran and Islam in his book *Tanqueeh Al-Abhath Fee Al-Milal Al-Thalaath* or *Refining Research in the Three Religions*.

In Waraqah Ibn Naufal's Quran, it seems paramount that the main goal was to unite all Jews and Christians under the new banner of Islam as shown in the following verse which has been repeated with different wordings with the same purport throughout the Quran:

"O People of the Scripture, Jews and Christians! Come to an agreement between us and you: that we all shall worship none but Allah."

(Aal-Omran, 64)

Another similar example from the Quran where Islam's mission seems to bring Jews and Christians into the fold of Islam is in the following relatively early verse of the Quran:

"O People of the Scripture (Jews and Christians), there has finally come to you Our Messenger (Muhammad) with a religion to show you righteousness and guidance." (Al-Maeda, 19)

Another more striking example from the Quran that bluntly states that Islam is the *Hanif*, Ebionites religion, namely, the Abrahamic religion, is the following verse that is often ignored by Muslim clerics who do not want the majority of ordinary Muslims to know the truth about Islam and the Quran:

"Say Allah has told the truth. So follow the religion of Abraham, Hanif (i.e. Ebionites); as he (Abraham) was not of the polytheists." (Aal-Omran, 95)

The verse is clearly commanding Muslims to follow the *Hanif* religion of Abraham (the Ebionites) unequivocally without any chance of ambiguity. The original Arabic version of this verse is even clearer than the English translation.

The Quran stressed that Islam takes its origin in the *Hanif* Ebionites religion as the basis of Islam. So another identical verse that calls for the *Hanif* religion unequivocally is the following verse:

"Abraham was neither a Jew nor a Christian but rather a Hanif (Ebionites) Muslim." (Aal-Omran, 67)

In this verse, the Quran unambiguously equalizes both *Hanif* religion with Islam, describing Abraham as a "*Hanif* Muslim." It is noteworthy to add that all Muslim clerics and preachers either shun this verse altogether or interpret *Hanif* as "Abraham a follower of Allah." Clerics hardly explain the *Hanif* religion or its real historical and religious meaning. Other clerics explain *Hanif* to mean "strong faith" even though there is nothing in the Arabic language to support this. The word *Hanif* does not have an Arabic root or even of an Arabic origin, but it is used to refer to the *Hanif* religion only in Arabic.

Moreover, Allah makes Jews and Christians unequivocally the only and exclusive reference and source for Muhammad for his new religion:

> *"So if you are in doubt, [O Muhammad], about that which We have revealed to you, then ask those who have been reading the Scripture before you. The truth has certainly come to you from your Lord, so never be among the doubters." (Yunis, 94)*

This verse in Yunis 94 proves that the Quran and Islam draw on a Jewish-Christian religion at heart and form, a further proof of Waraqah's Ebionites mission.

Waraqah Ibn Naufal was a highly educated scholar and very knowledgeable about Judaism and Christianity. He was well-read in ancient history and the old religions of the world. He got a lot of wealth and power in his tribe in Mecca. He was also a distant uncle of Muhammad. More importantly, he was the first cousin of Khadijah, Muhammad's first wife and longest marriage. The details of the marriage and the role of Ibn Naufal in writing the Quran are all outlined in *Al-Seerah Al-Nabawiyah* or *The Prophet's Biography* by Ibn Hisham (Died in 833 AD).

Khadijah was a very rich lady in Mecca, and she hired young Muhammad who was her junior by 15 years. She put him in charge of her wealth while Waraqah Ibn Naufal was closely watching Muhammad's every step. After an initial trust-building period and by virtue of Muhammad's righteousness and honesty, Khadijah proposed to Muhammad. Yes, Muhammad himself and all Muslim references corroborate this unusual and possibly unprecedented act in Arabia. Obviously that was the initial plan to bring Muhammad in and groom him for his larger-than-life, historical mission, to be the prophet of Islam.

Waraqah Ibn Naufal was the priest that officiated the marriage contract following the Christian Ebionites tradition. Khadijah (circa 555 - 619 AD) was Ebionite herself. Therefore, Muhammad's marriage with Khadijah was essentially a Christian marriage, and that explains why Muhammad stayed monogamous as divorce or having more than one wife was not allowed to the Christian Ebionites. It was only when Waraqah Ibn Naufal and Khadijah died that Muhammad, being a powerful rich leader by then, could marry an additional twelve women and children (Aieshah was under nine years old when he married her) within a very short period (about twelve years before he died in 632 AD) compared to the time when he stayed married to Khadijah which lasted about twenty-five years.

Another indication of Waraqah's role in Islam is that the legendary influence of Waraqah Ibn Naufal upon Muhammad and his Quran abruptly stopped when aging Waraqah died (see *Sahih Al-Bukhari*, 1/38). It is neither surprising nor accidental then that Muhammad's companions noticed that "revelations ceased for a long time" following the death of Waraqah. All Islamic sources admit unmistakably that there was a "dry period of two years" right after the death of Waraqah Ibn Naufal (see *Sahih Al-Bukhari* 1/38).

The reason, of course, is that Muhammad was no longer receiving verses or texts of the Quran from his Ebionite uncle. Luckily for Muhammad, another Ebionite scholar and cleric named Rahib Behery filled in after two years of no Quran supply and when he took over, the delivery of the Quran resumed.

It is equally important to mention that it is very clear that there is a huge and instantly recognizable difference in style, diction, and content between the Quran of the Waraqah period and the Quran of Behery period that can be pointed out by even the least trained eye.

Historically, it is evident that Waraqah Ibn Naufal messed up the whole course of humanity by playing the most dangerous game (or rather the nastiest trick) in the history of mankind. He convinced or scared Muhammad into believing that he was Allah's Prophet and supplied him with what he called the Book of Allah, The Quran. To be fair, the Quran has lots of good material that regulates people's daily life in a sophisticated manner. However, to convince people and to rally followers, there is an equal amount of intimidation and abuse in the Quran as well. In other words, the Quran is full of many unconscionable parts that call for violence and abuse.

Did Waraqah Ibn Naufal plan to take over once Muhammad succeeds and Islam becomes an established religion? No. Unquestionably, Waraqah Ibn Naufal was a much older man than Muhammad. He was about forty years older. Definitely, there is no claim to the idea that Waraqah wanted to capture the new budding leadership. Obviously, he only wanted a harmonious religion that would accommodate for everyone in the two big religions, Judaism and Christianity. It is ironical that this idealistic, Don Quixotic plan not just fired back but blew up in the face of all mankind.

Waraqah Ibn Naufal was a poet and that explains the poetic nature of the Quran. He was deeply knowledgeable of the Talmud, the Old Testament, and the New Testament and that explains the generous amount of plagiarism of large amounts of stories and parts from previous religions into the Quran. In *Kitab Al-Aghani*, 3/113 by Abu Al-Farag Al-Asfahani (Died 967 AD) and in *Al-Isharat Al-Ilahiyah* by Abu Hayan Al-Tauheedi (Died 1023 AD), there are clear references to Ibn Naufal's use of the Old Testament in the Quran.

Ibn Naufal was keen on steering people from the beliefs of the Roman Church that Jesus is the Son of God and that explains why the Quran and Islam are against the idea that Jesus being the Son of God, i.e. Jesus' divinity.

Another pressing question is to which side does Islam lean more: to Judaism or to Christianity? Since Islam follows, to a great extent, the Law of Moses and since Islam denies the divinity of Jesus to the degree that Muslims sacrifice every year in a holy ceremony a lamb which indicates the denial of Jesus being the sacrifice for human sin, then a pondered view indicates that Islam is more of a Jewish religion than a Christian one. The history of the Ebionites and the fact that Waraqah Ibn Naufal was Ebionite all point to that direction too. Does that mean radicals like Jews? Absolutely no. the radical brand of Islam is an ideology of control, not for human brotherhood or love. Radicals see both Jews and Christians as arch enemies of Islam and they use inopportunely many verses from the Quran to support their hatred. On the other hand, moderate peaceful Muslims who are the sweeping majority of Muslims do not feel the same as radicals. Moderate Muslims love all.

Chapter Twelve

Waraqah's Quran VS Uthman's Quran

Prophet Muhammad died in June 632 AD at the age of 62. Before his death, he confirmed that the Quran was complete and that his mission had been completed even though the Quran itself had not been recorded down or registered at all except for few verses on animal hides, paper, palm tree fronds, wood, and rocks. The Quran was mainly memorized by the prophet's companions. There was no complete, compiled codex of the Quran by the time Muhammad died.

The first Khalif, Abu Bakr, ordered in 634 AD (few months before his death) the first written compilation of the Quran as "revealed" or "given" to Muhammad by Waraqah and Behery. Abu Bakr sources were the prophet's companions and the few fragmentary written verses on animal hides, rocks, paper, palm tree fronds, and wood. After the compilation was done, Abu Bakr right before he died left what he compiled with Hafsah, the Prophet Muhammad's widow. Abu Bakr's move to collect the Quran into that codex (called Hafsah's Codex because she was the one who kept it) was mainly because many of the prophet's companions who memorized the Quran were dying in scores either naturally or in battles. This first version of the Quran (Hafsah's Codex) is actually Muhammad's Quran (or more specifically Waraqah's) as he concluded it; however, it was destroyed afterward, specifically, after Hafsah's death (as it will be explained later in this chapter) under certain historical circumstances that entailed such action and replaced by another version.

By the time of the third Khalif, Uthman Ibn Affan (he ruled for twelve years from 644 to 656 AD, when he was killed), most of the prophet's companions who memorized the Quran were dead by then. Uthman ordered the rewriting of the Quran again. However, there was another historically important reason that triggered Uthman to have a new version of the Quran beside the death of the prophet's companions. This reason will shed light on the authenticity of the Quran itself.

***

The historical reason according to Islamic sources was that Hudhaifa (one Muslim military leader) came to Uthman and expressed his deep concern about the differences in the Quran: According to Sahih Bukhary (Vol. 6- Book 61- Page 10):

"Hudhaifa was afraid of the different recitations of the Qur'an, so he asked Uthman, "O chief of the Believers! Save this nation before they differ about the Qur'an as Jews and the Christians did before."

From that quote, it is clear that there were different versions of the Quran already and by the admission of documents at the time and a consensus of all Islamic sources that this incident occurred; one wonders which Quran Uthman adopted.

Right after the killing of Uthman (656 AD), when arguments were raised about the original Quran (also known as Muhammad's Quran, or Waraqah's Quran or Hafsah's Codex) and its differences from Uthman's Quran, Marwan Ibn Al-Hakam, the governor of Medina, (b. 623 - d. 685 AD) realized the drastic differences between the original one and Uthman's copy. The big problem then was that Uthman had already, years before his death, sent three copies to Egypt, Iraq, and Syria and the fourth is presumed to have been kept in Medina. So what did Marwan Ibn Al-Hakam do? He ordered the original Quran taken from Hafsah's home right after her death (Hafsah was born 602 - died 661 AD), and Marwan Ibn Al-Hakam had that original Quran destroyed, definitely fearing it would become the cause of terrible disputes and probably the disintegration of the Islamic state. He feared that people would find out the differences and the contradictions between the original Quran and Uthman's Quran.

Today, the question is how extensive are the differences between a Quran written by Waraqah Ibn Naufal, adopted by Muhammad (the original Quran), compiled by Abu Bakr, kept by Hafsah, and burnt by Marwan Ibn Al-Hakam on one hand and the Quran of Uthman on the other hand? No one would believe or just imagine the differences because Hafsah's Codex was destroyed long ago. However, it turned out that some of the few first fragmentary manuscripts of the Quran written during Muhammad's life which never exceeded more than 800 verses recorded on animal hides and palm tree branches have survived.

The writer of this book had the unique opportunity to see some manuscripts that survived time and intrigue. I had a very rare opportunity to see four old twisted pieces of sheep hides where a total of 89 verses were inscribed during a visit to a chief of a tribe in Al-Taief region in the early summer of 2010. I could read the content easily even though there were no dots used on the letters of Arabic. The major difference between written classical Arabic and written modern Arabic is the use of dots in addition to sharp, angular letters unlike modern Arabic where letters have dots and are more curvy and have relatively more rounded edges. However, that was not a problem to the writer of this book, being a veteran linguist and researcher, to read the manuscripts with fair ease.

I was trembling while I held the manuscripts in my hands. I repeatedly asked for how long the tribe and the successive chiefs have had these manuscripts. I also wondered if they were keeping them secretly. They affirmed it is a big secret to keep them and it could cost them their lives just declaring that they are in possession of those manuscripts.

The hides were yellowish to tawny in color, very hardened and I could see some erosion on some spots, almost paper-thin because of time and the elements. They were kept in a big wooden box in a room underground. The whole experience was eerie and I could see that my hosts were very nervous and anxious. I examined the manuscripts carefully and I felt my hands were starting to sweat, so I placed the manuscript on a desk in the room. Out of breath, even though I did not move much, I started examining the manuscripts that should change the history of mankind forever.

On one of the sheep hides, the Quran verses were inscribed as follows:

"To Allah belongs whatever is in the heavens and whatever is on the earth. And to Allah will [all] matters be returned.
You are the best nation produced [as an example] for mankind. You command what is right and abstain from what is wrong and believe in Allah. If only the People of the Scripture had believed, it would have been better for them.
Among them are believers. Among the People of the Scripture is a group standing [in obedience], reciting the verses of Allah during periods of the night and prostrating as they pray. They believe in Allah and the Last Day, and they command what is right and abstain from what is wrong and hasten to good deeds. And those are among the righteous. And whatever good they do - never will it be taken away from them. And Allah is Knowing of the righteous." (Al-Taief Document 1)

The above text is the exact wording of the verses. However, in the official Quran of Uthman which is the present-day Quran, the verses go differently with a large portion interpolated. The official Quran of today goes like this:

"To Allah belongs whatever is in the heavens and whatever is on the earth. And to Allah will [all] matters be returned.
You are the best nation produced [as an example] for mankind. You command what is right and abstain from what is wrong and believe in Allah. If only the People of the Scripture had believed, it would have been better for them. Among them are believers, *but most of them are defiantly disobedient. They will not harm you except for [some] annoyance. And if they fight you, they will show you their backs; then they will not be aided. They have been put*

under humiliation [by Allah] wherever they are overtaken, except for a covenant from Allah and a rope from the Muslims. And they have drawn upon themselves anger from Allah and have been put under destitution. That is because they disbelieved in the verses of Allah and killed the prophets without right. That is because they disobeyed and [habitually] transgressed. They are not [all] the same; among the People of the Scripture is a group standing [in obedience], reciting the verses of Allah during periods of the night and prostrating as they pray. They believe in Allah and the Last Day, and they command what is right and abstain from what is wrong and hasten to good deeds. And those are among the righteous. And whatever good they do - never will it be removed from them. And Allah is Knowing of the righteous." (Aal-Omran, 109-115)

It is clear that the italicized portion is not in line with the rest of the text. There is a noticeable incongruity in meaning. Also the theme of the people of the Scripture is praised before and after the italicized portion; meaning flows more naturally in the text that I read in Al-Taief. Basically, the tone is reconciliatory towards the people of the Scriptures, i.e., Jews and Christians in the text of Al-Taief, while it is highly aggressive in the Uthman's version. So it is clear that there is an interpolated part in present-day Uthman Quran, and this part does not belong thematically at all. It simply does not fit in meaning or context.

***

Moreover, and more convincing is that the original verses I read in Al-Taief agree with other similar reconciliatory, ingratiatory, mild-toned verses in the Quran such as:

"Indeed, those who believed and those who were Jews or Christians or Sabeans [before Prophet Muhammad] - those [among them] who believed in Allah and the Last Day and did righteousness - will have their reward with their Lord, and no fear will there be concerning them, nor will they grieve." (Al-Baqara, 62)

And this agrees also with another reconciliatory, ingratiatory verse:

"O People of the Scripture, Jews and Christians! Come to an agreement between us and you: that we all shall worship none but Allah."

(Aal-Omran, 64)

Therefore, my conclusion is that there is an immense Quran change and there are a lot of thematic and ideational contradictions in the present-day Quran.

Moreover, I examined another animal skin piece in a relatively the same condition as the first one, and when I read the manuscript, I could easily see another obvious interpolation in Uthman's version which is in use today by Muslims. The old manuscript read:

"Say, We (Muslims) have believed in Allah and in what was revealed to us and what was revealed before to Abraham, Ishmael, Isaac, Jacob, and the Descendants, and in what was given to Moses and Jesus and to all the prophets from their Lord. We make no distinction between any of them, and we are submitting to Him. How shall Allah guide a people who disbelieved after their belief and had witnessed that the Messenger is true and clear signs had come to them? And Allah does not guide the wrongdoing people." (Al-Taief Document 2)

***

However, the present day official Quran compiled by Uthman shows a different version:

"Say, We (Muslims) have believed in Allah and in what was revealed to us and what was revealed before to Abraham, Ishmael, Isaac, Jacob, and the Descendants, and in what was given to Moses and Jesus and to all the prophets from their Lord. We make no distinction between any of them, and we are submitting to Him. *And whoever desires other than Islam as religion - never will it be accepted from him, and he, in the Hereafter, will be among the losers.* How shall Allah guide a people who disbelieved after their belief and had witnessed that the Messenger is true and clear signs had come to them? And Allah does not guide the wrongdoing people."

(Aal-Omran, 84-86)

Again, there was no part in the manuscript that I read that had the italicized portion. There is a sudden change of subject and theme with the interpolated part. In other words, it is out of sync with the verses before and after and even contradicts many other verses in the Quran where, for example, the prophet simply says people are free to believe in whatever they want.

***

So why did Uthman do that? The answer is in modern day politics as well as the time of Uthman himself. There was fear and a perceived challenge from Jews and Christians to the new religion of Islam, and as we see in our modern times, Israel and the West are a scapegoat for all the dysfunction of the vast Islamic world; Uthman also felt the same. He felt the Islamic state was threatened by the Jews and Christians living in Arabia (present-day Saudi Arabia) and the Christian Roman Empire, in both Rome and Constantinople (the Byzantines) north and west of the Islamic state (present-day Italy and Turkey). It was convenient for him to interpolate some anti-Christian and anti-Jewish verses to secure his state and to justify taking the lands of the Christians in Syria, Palestine, Egypt, and Lebanon which were all under Christian rule as well as justify the killing of all Jews and Christians living in Arabia at that time. However, it is hoped that radical Muslims would show little humbleness and some humility after they know what their religion is about and learn the truth of the Quran.

Chapter Thirteen

Reform and Enlightenment by Muslim Philosophers and Intellectuals

From day one, Islam was rejected by many and the consequences were not pleasant at all as I explained in Chapter Eight the horror that Muslims inflicted on those who opposed it. In almost every country invaded by Muslims, there were a lot of atrocities and massacres of the conquered peoples. Therefore, some intellectuals decided to take on Islam rationally. For that purpose, intellectuals fought Islam using a weapon that Islam could not destroy: Reason. In every country or land subjugated by Muslims, and during every decade since Islam struck, there had been more than one intellectual who tried to enlighten his people and use all possible logic and reason to reveal the clandestine deception and the subtle pretence in the theology of the Islamic faith and doctrine.

Among the hundreds of philosophers, freethinkers, and intellectuals who lived and grew up under Muslim domination, I chose five remarkable figures. They represent different periods of time and they used different philosophical approaches and methods in their attempt to reform Islam and enlighten the Muslims. They also come from different parts of the Islamic world.

They are Al-Farabi, also known as Alpharabius (b. 872 - d. 950 AD), Ibn Sina, also known as Avicenna (b. 980 - d. 1037 AD), Ibn Rushd, also known as Averroes (b. 1126 - d.

1198 AD), Taha Hussein (b. 1889 - d. 1973), and Nasr Hamid Abu Zayd (b. 1943 - d. 2010).

What is common amongst these great figures is that each was a scholar of tremendous and varied learning and deep knowledge in science, philosophy, medicine, linguistics, theology, physics, chemistry, psychology, and literature. Furthermore, these philosophers sought to reconcile rigid Islamic theology with rational approaches that would renew Islamic thought. *Ijtihad* is an important term in Islamic scholarship which means the rational practice in Islamic theology that seeks to consider any claim in the Quranic text in a new light and use reason in interpreting the Quran; and that was what these remarkable philosophers and hundreds others tried to do to reform Islam.

***

Al-Farabi was a great scientist, philosopher, and logician acknowledged in the East and West alike for his great works and commentaries on Aristotle. He adopted the Aristotelian logic and metaphysics theories in order to explain the discrepancies in Islamic theology in an indirect way as he feared for his life in case he approached the contradictions of the Quran directly, or openly criticised the Quran. Instead, he used inference, both Aristotelian and non-Aristotelian to reach conclusions about the verity of Quranic content and claims. He simply divided logic and logical perception of facts into two groups: "idea" and "proof." By separating logic and logical perception into two categories, Al-Farabi shrewdly and intelligently tried to make Muslims understand and realize that not every ideational entity told to them in the Quran can be true as long as "proof" is lacking because logic entails both "idea" and "proof."

Al-Farabi went even further to enlighten the Muslims by depicting religion in a new light. To do so, he wrote a remarkable book titled *Al-Madina Al-Fadila,* which can be translated as the *Utopia* or *The Virtuous City*. He simply presented religion as a Neoplatonic symbol rather than a real revelation from a Higher Being. To Al-Farabi, religion was a Neoplatonic concept which meant it was rhetoric rather than Quranic metaphysics (metaphysics is the branch of philosophy and science that deals with the limits of human knowledge, existence, and origin of the universe). Instead, as mentioned earlier, Al-Farabi adopted Aristotle's Neoplatonic metaphysics instead of the Quranic explanation of the universe, existence, afterlife, punishment and human knowledge. In other words, his Neoplatonic book, *Al-Madina Al-Fadila,* was an attempt to make Muslims see religion and the universe from a different point of view rather than the Quran's depiction. He used adroitly for this purpose logic, philosophy, and indirect symbolism in his book *Al-Madina Al-Fadila.*

To illustrate what he did in the book, Al-Farabi described humans in the universe as standing between two spheres: a higher, intellectual, celestial one and a lower, material, decaying one. This description of humans is not the one of the Quran at all. He intentionally adopted a completely new view different from the mainstream Islamic view. Furthermore, he said that in the hereafter, only the perfect intellect would survive after death, the body is annihilated altogether. Again this is not what the Quran states or portrays in its verses.

It is not surprising that Al-Farabi believed that the role of the philosopher in society is similar to the physician to the body of a sick patient. According to him, a philosopher has a role to perform in healing his society. On the whole, Al-Farabi tried to fuse Aristotle's logic with Plato's philosophy regarding the creation of the universe, survival of the intellect, the afterlife, paradise, punishment, etc., in a way different from that of the Quran with a view to changing Muslims perception of the Quran itself. Al-Farabi travelled all over the Islamic world, from modern day Afghanistan, Iran, Syria, Iraq, and Egypt and to everywhere in-between diligently trying to heal his Muslim society.

***

Like Al-Farabi, Avicenna adopted the Aristotelian logic and metaphysics and explained further the impossibility of the Quranic configuration of the world as presented in the Quran. He was a bit more daring than Al-Farabi. Avicenna concluded that angels and Jin (spirits and ghosts) could not be true the way they were depicted in the Quran. He completely denied on logical grounds that angels and spirits could act the way they were presented in the Quran. He also added that logically the description of paradise, hell, and the hereafter as presented in the Quran are mere envisions of the prophet Muhammad rather than an accurate indication of their existence. By doing so, Avicenna demolished the Quranic authenticity and holiness which are the major factors used in attracting people to Islam through materialistic and physical appeal.

Moreover, and like his teacher, Al-Farabi, whom he never met but read all his works, Avicenna asserted that the universe was not created but rather it is eternal; this idea brings down the whole Islamic theology that sees Allah as the creator of the universe. He further asserted that only the soul can be resurrected while the body is annihilated. This is counter to the Quranic teachings that lure people to faith for sensual pleasures in paradise. In that attempt, Avicenna tried to limit the scope of Muslims' imagination of the afterlife and simultaneously describing a universe that is more logical rather than one based on rhetoric.

Avicenna asserted also that Allah's knowledge is limited. This is a natural conclusion since the soul, Avicenna affirms, is free and not controlled, and its actions are not predicted. While the Quran in several verses says that "Allah knows what is in your hearts" and that "Allah is omniscient of your souls," Avicenna says "how that can be if the soul cannot be tracked and that its freedom is absolute." Humans have a free will, Avicenna emphasised that fact based on his ontological observations and conclusions which is counter to the Quran verses.

Aristotelian metaphysics was a major source of Avicenna's philosophy. He explained that knowledge is available to everyone, not just prophets. Therefore, Avicenna equalized philosophers with prophets. He put philosophers and prophets on the same epistemological footing. Even further, he asserted that there are no more prophets since Muhammad was the last prophet as Islam and the Quran affirm. Avicenna said that Muhammad had more knowledge at his time and, therefore, he was more knowledgeable than philosophers. However, philosophers are continuing to pursue after knowledge and they continue in increasing their knowledge unlike prophets who died and never come back. In saying so, Avicenna gave philosophers the upper hand and a great advantage over prophets in that philosophers' knowledge is updated and renewable. This was exceptionally revolutionary to say by Avicenna.

***

A major enemy of Islamic reform was Al-Ghazali (b. 1058 - d.1111 AD). His efforts in impeding any Islamic renaissance were palpable during his life time and after, perhaps until the present day. He inspired others such as Ibn Taymiyyah, Mohammad Ibn Abdel Wahab, Hassan Al-Banna, Sayed Qutb and many others to block any attempt of reforming Islam. Al-Ghazali in particular was exceptionally an impediment to Islamic scientific advancement. Before him, Islamic scholarship reached its highest point and the Islamic civilization surpassed Europe and all Eastern civilizations, but thanks to him and to his preaching and teachings, the Islamic world deteriorated to its lowest point in the history of human civilization.

Al-Ghazali antagonized himself against philosophy and any rational thinking. He rejected Greek and Roman philosophy. He says that when he studied philosophy, he just learned about its "deception and ambiguity." He then adds that philosophers are "marked by non-belief and atheism." He declared Al-Farabi and Avicenna apostates and atheists for their adoption of the Hellenistic way of thought and methods.

Al-Ghazali placed Islamic theology above Hellenistic thought and rationalism. In doing so, Islam lost a golden opportunity to remain a class world civilization. Despite all attempts after Al-Ghazali's death to revive rational thinking by Averroes and many others, Al-Ghazali's influence was devastating enough to Islam and world civilization. His negative influence was far more reaching than any possible reform.

Al-Ghazali wrote *The Incoherence of Philosophers* in which he rejected skepticism and logical thinking and particularly attacked Avicenna. He referred all knowledge of the universe to Allah's knowledge and will alone. He affirmed that humans have no will but only Allah's will that moves the universe as the Quran describes. In saying so, then, philosophy and rationalism were rendered redundant. In his book, Al-Ghazali condemned all Greek philosophers as well as Muslim philosophers and characterized them as danger to the Islamic faith for using methods and techniques of thinking counter to the Quran and Muhammad's teachings.

***

Despite Al-Ghazali's heavy-handed condemnation of rationalism, another attempt and a forceful one came from another great polymath and philosopher who enlightened the twelfth century, namely, Averroes. He did his best to revive philosophy and rationalism. He supported Aristotelian philosophy against Islamic theology. First, he tried to do damage control after Al-Ghazali deformed philosophy and defamed philosophers. So Averroes wrote *The Incoherence of The Incoherence* as a rebuttal to Al-Ghazali's *The Incoherence of Philosophers*. Thus, Averroes set out in his book to prove that Al-Ghazali's argument against philosophy and rationalism was faulty since he (Al-Ghazali) was using Islamic criteria to judge Aristotelian logic. In that, Al-Ghazali was completely off mark, Averroes argued. He further said that rationalism could not be judged by irrationalism which Al-Ghazali did in his attack on philosophy. Furthermore, Averroes said that Al-Ghazali is wrong because he (Al-Ghazali) assumed that there is one interpretation of the Quran; as a matter of fact, the scripture, Averroes affirms, is open to interpretation as time passes and as different people reflect on it and read it.

***

Averroes second important book was *Fasl Al-Maqal*. When extremists tried to shut down Averroes to the extent of convincing the Andalusian ruler, Abu Yaqub Yousef, to put Averroes in jail or exile him for his atheism and his attempts to corrupt Islamic theology, Averroes wrote *Fasl Al-Maqal* in which he explained the need to philosophy and logic, and that rationalism and religion are not incompatible. Therefore, he argued that prohibiting philosophy was unnecessary. He further explained that religious proof and evidence are incomplete and incapable of reaching the truth; hence, philosophy is needed.

Averroes stated that the religious text is open to interpretation; there should be no rigid meaning to the scripture so much so that when meaning is incompatible with actual truth, the scripture should be interpreted allegorically and metaphorically. In another book titled *Kashf Aan Al-Manahij* or *Revealing the Methods*, Averroes argues that when one explores the personal doctrines of the masses and comparing them to the different sects of the time, he concludes that there is a lot of distortion and discrepancies in people's interpretations and beliefs because people or the "masses" use methods and approaches of thinking that are far from rational or even sensible.

Unfortunately, despite the revival of rationalism in the twelfth century, Islamic reform was dealt another blow by Ibn Taymiyyah's rise a century later. Ibn Taymiyyah is considered the one Islamic theologian who introduced radical, extremist Islam in the fourteenth century which has survived till today.

Ironically, Muslim rationalists such as Al-Farabi, Avicenna, and Averroes left their big impact not on the Islamic world but on Europe and Western thought. Europe's Renaissance definitely owes its success to Muslim rationalists and philosophers. The West benefited a great deal from Islamic rationalism. Unfortunately, the same did not happen to Muslims. Muslim reformers' influence reached all European thinkers and universities while the Islamic world was sinking into darkness and backwardness thanks to Ibn Taymiyyah.

It was not until the late nineteenth century and the twentieth century when the next wave of Muslim rationalists and intellectuals who tried to reform Islam had arrived. Taha Hussein was one remarkable figure. He fought many battles at every arena, in courts, in the press, as a writer, and in academia to rid Islam of elements that caused Muslims' backwardness in the twentieth century. He suffered a lot as a result but he succeeded in stirring many controversies that brought about palpable awakening.

He tackled many presumed ideas that were taken for granted for so long such as the stories told in the Quran. For example, he pointed out that there was no evidence that Abraham and Ishmael could have come to Arabia as the Quran says. He added that it was a ruse by Muhammad to convince the people of Arabia that Islam is a continuation of Judaism and thus bring Jews into Islam voluntarily. The fact that Taha Hussein tackled this subject in this manner and casting doubt on the Quran was unprecedented and for the first time in nine centuries, since Averroes, Muslims hear someone rejecting the Quran's authenticity. Taha Hussein talked bluntly about constants of the Quran as mere mythological stories rather than Allah's revelation to his prophet Muhammad.

The most important book that Taha Hussein wrote was *Pre-Islamic Poetry* (1926 AD). The impact of that book was far more reaching than any other book that tried to press for Islamic reform in the first half of the twentieth century. Taha Hussein basically affirmed in his book that pre-Islamic poetry diction, style, the description of the ways of life of the people of Arabia, and the subjects discussed were similar and almost cognate to those of the Quran. He then concluded that they (i.e., the Quran and the presumed pre-Islamic poetry) must have been written at the same time or that the presumed pre-Islamic poetry was actually written much later after the Quran was written.

***

He concludes further that what is called pre-Islamic poetry was in fact falsified and wrongly attributed to pre-Islamic poets to pre-empt any doubt about the Quran. It was a kind of cover-up, Hussein affirms. Why is this significant? There is a serious implication made by Taha Hussein which is that the Quran is a human product and that its style is no more than the writing of a good poet, and not Allah's holy word. If the Quran's style and diction are similar to poetry, then the Quran is not a linguistic miracle as radical Muslims claim.

As a result, Muslim Extremists at the time were so angry that they took Taha Hussein to court and had the book banned and had Taha Hussein fired later from his academic career as a professor at the University of Cairo.

When Taha Hussein was in charge of education in 1950 and under a new government, he introduced significant changes to the education system in Egypt. He ordered all education from elementary level to university level to be free. He made sure that all education will be available to all, poor and rich. He is also credited for scaling back and finally shutting down Islamic religious schools (Kottab) and replaced them with secular general education schools all over Egypt.

Taha Hussein also supported the revival of Ancient Pharaonic civilization since it was overtaken by the invading Islamic armies. He also stressed that the Quran should not be considered a reliable source of history. These claims were daring and meant to weaken the hegemony of the Islamic theology and ways of thinking that were prevalent all over Egypt and the Islamic world. For this reason, he called upon fundamentalists and traditional theologians to think anew and revise their beliefs and pursue *Ijtihad*, i.e. reform and thinking of new ways to study the Quran from an objective and a rational perspective.

***

The next reformist was Nasr Hamid Abu Zayd who had a forthright approach against traditional Islamic theology. He openly demanded a new reading of the Quran unlike his intellectual predecessors. He applied Hermeneutics' standards and principles in the analysis of the Quran. Hermeneutics in simple terms may be defined as the analysis and interpretation of a text for itself regardless of any subjective factors, no matter how holy these factors might be. And in applying that to the Quran, Muslims, Abu Zayd affirms, will learn more about the truth of the Quran as well as the cultural and historical circumstances of its writing. In other words, the Quran, Abu Zayd says, should be treated as an ordinary text, not a holy one, when it comes to analysing it.

Furthermore, Abu Zayd rejected the Quran as the dominant religious scripture in the Arabic culture, and demanded treating it as a regular text and that it should be studied within the context of its appearance at the start of the sixth century. That directly indicated, according to Abu Zayd, that the Quran is not a universal, eternal text that supersedes time and place.

Radical Muslims claim the Quran is eternal, written by Allah. For Abu Zayd to say that the Quran is not eternal was a big blow to radicals and voids its authenticity as a holy book revealed by Allah. He further affirmed that the dominance of the Quran held back the Arabic culture and prevented it from advancement.

Abu Zayd was also critical of many verses of the Quran as being inhumane to minorities living under Muslims' rule or for being too irrational. For example, he denounced the Quran for imposing a special tax called "Jizyah" on non-Muslims, specifically, Christians and Jews living in Muslim lands. Abu Zayd described this tax as an instance of unequal treatment of fellow human beings.

It is important to mention that all the rationalists introduced in this chapter and almost all other rationalists and reformists were persecuted, declared apostates, imprisoned or exiled and hunted down for their beliefs and their attempts to advance their Islamic societies.

However, the rationalist movement led by intellectuals such as Al-Farabi, Avicenna, Averroes, Taha Hussein and Nasr Abu Zayd has generated bigger waves of intellectuals across the Islamic world. They definitely inspired millions with the need to reform Islam. Although intellectuals today are carrying the torch to enlighten Muslims, there are those who are trying to put it out and spread a blanket of ignorance to prevent light from shining. The light has not spread yet to all parts of the Islamic world, but one day, it would prevail over darkness.

Chapter Fourteen

Sharia and Breast Feeding

According to strict interpretation of *Sharia* (Islamic law), a man cannot mingle with or see a woman to whom he is not related as a father, son, brother father in-law, or husband. Any other man is considered illegitimate to see a woman's face. So how modern-day Muslims would get around that law? In 2010 an ultra-conservative cleric in Saudi Arabia issued a *fatwa* (a religious decree) stating that an adult man can suckle from an adult woman's breast and that would render him "a breast-fed brother" to that woman, and thus he can see her face or mingle with her in public. There is a basis for this in Sharia that simply states that no one can marry a woman whom he shared with the same "breast milk even a drop." By the same token, an unrelated adult male (i.e. not a father or son, etc.), can drink a woman's breast milk and that would establish a mother-son bond in Islamic tradition.

The cleric's name was Sheik Abdul-Mohsen al-Obeikan. The *fatwa* caused uproar as it meant a stranger needs to approach a woman and ask her to suckle from her breast. After few drops, they become related by "milk." It was even bizarre to know this is an old established rule and practice in Islamic law, but the way the cleric suggested it was ridiculous and luckily led to his dismissal from his position in the high orders of the religious circles in Riyadh. His reasoning was deemed simply preposterous.

When I brought up this issue in class during a composition exercise, there were two trends among students: one conservative group that refused the way the media handled the issue as it weakens the image of Islam since the media described the practice as a public suckling session while in fact it would be done in the privacy of a person's home whereas the other view of the second group was that it was acceptable and the Sheik or cleric was right. They facetiously liked the breast suckling practice, and they saw nothing wrong with that. However, no student thought it was ridiculous in any way. The students said the Sheik should have been rewarded for his ingenuity and service to the men and women of Islam. The students affirmed that the fatwa was a big boost to curb illegitimate mingling which is strictly forbidden in Islam.

I really did not understand their reasoning because it was very preposterous to think that way, and I knew I had a tremendous task, if not entirely impossible to change the students' way of thinking. It is true that Islam is a religion of convenience. This means that a Muslim would look for and find a text in the Quran or *Sunnah* (the prophet's sayings and practices) that either directly addresses a certain issue or, if not, the text would be interpreted the way a person wants it and that is all they need to do, and in that way, they solve their theological problems and sticky issues by getting a fatwa or crafting a convenient interpretation of the Quran or Sunnah.

Chapter Fifteen

The Suspicion of Praying to another God

In late 2011 and early 2012, there were reports of arrests made of Saudis and foreigners who were caught in their homes for praying; crosses and Bibles were found as proof of their practicing Christianity. Moreover, there was a big case touted in Saudi newspapers and TV channels of "thirty-five Ethiopian Christians" who were taken into custody by Saudi authorities. The charge was setting up Christian worship in one of the homes of the Ethiopians. "They were appallingly caught praying to Jesus Christ in the Land of Muhammad," the TV announcer said triumphantly the other night. I could not help weeping for the poor Ethiopians when I heard the news.

The Saudi authorities apparently forgot that the Land of Muhammad was originally inhabited by Jews, Christians, and polytheists before Muhammad and his followers usurped the land in the seventh century.

***

The news and newspapers highlighted that most of the Ethiopian detainees were women and children. American and European Human Rights organizations tried to help legally and sent letters to King Abdullah. The detainees reported to a lawyer hired by the US

Human Rights Watch that they were strip-searched, beaten, tortured, taunted for being "infidels," and sexually abused by police. Two women detainees reported that the police inserted their fingers into their vaginas in search for drugs.

Another preposterous charge brought up against the Ethiopian Christian worshippers was "illegal mingling" which means that the men and women caught worshipping in that private home were not related to each other by marriage or blood. According to Saudi and Islamic law, men and women who are not related by blood or marriage are forbidden from "mingling together" and meant they were also charged of committing "vice," i.e. sexual promiscuity.

Saudi law also bans the practice of any religion other than Islam; although in 2006, Saudi authorities declared, under international pressure, that it would allow the practice of other religions, yet this incident and many others prove that there is no reform whatsoever and religious intolerance continues against their Saudi citizens and foreigners alike.

Chapter Sixteen

An Australian's Torture and Sharia

There was a case of an Australian who was accused of blasphemy. A horrible charge in Saudi Arabia and most Muslim countries where extremists rule. Punishment can be anything from jail time, lashings and beating as a form of torture, and up to the death penalty.

So what did that poor Australian actually do or say? The local news outlets reported "he insulted the prophet Muhammad's companions." Other news sources claim the Australian made "degrading remarks about the prophet himself."

The prophet's companions are partly disciples and partly allies and believers or simply they were those who believed and supported the prophet's mission as a messenger of Allah during his life time. Anyone who cast doubt on Muhammad's prophecy or did not support the prophet was dubbed infidel by Muhammad and his followers and companions. That is why the prophet companions are held in high esteem in the Islamic faith. They learned the Quran by rote, and they narrated all the prophet's day-to-day activities and, therefore, they are the primary source of all Islamic jurisprudence regarding, for example, what the prophet would do when this or that situation happened. It is all as told by the companions.

Moreover, the prophet companions are held in high esteem for many other reasons during Muhammad's time and after. They not only supported Muhammad but helped spread the religion after his death. They were also, so to speak, his biographers and emissaries many decades after Muhammad's death. Therefore, they are accredited in the history of Islam for the vital role in sustaining Muhammad's mission to serve "Allah's cause." One may partly think of them as Jesus disciples except that the disciples were very small in number. Muhammad's companions reach twelve hundred in number as one Muslim scholar noted to me.

The poor Australian was a Muslim convert who tried to fit in his new religion and naively, he asked questions in the way we would do in the West. In the Muslim culture, questioning borders on doubting, a practice that is scowled upon. One has to take the whole of the Islamic religion with all its obscure teachings for an outsider as is without doubt; total blind faith as one Muslim friend explained to me. "The rule is: believe first and all your questions will disappear, but don't start with asking and doubting. It is not a good sign of true belief in the heart," my Muslim friend explained to me. He then asked "Are you planning to become a Muslim? Many people do."

"No, no," I replied categorically and emphatically. "At least not now as I'm still learning first."

A weird issue about converting to Islam is that once one declares himself or herself a Muslim, one cannot go back. One cannot get out of that religion of Islam once one embraces it. If one does try to get out, then the penalty is killing. A simple rule for the religion of peace. Equally, once one is born Muslim to a family of Muslims, it goes without saying, that one cannot leave the religion, or death will be the penalty. It is not in our Western culture where one is having full freedom of religion in the full sense of freedom of choice.

At the end, Tim and I learned that the Australian was sentenced to a year in prison and five hundred mix of cane and whip lashes on his back beside all the abuse and taunting from other inmates; we also learned that the Australian died in jail and was given a good Muslim burial "since he was cleansed of his sins by the fair punishment, he died a good Muslim," the authorities of the local prison said.

Sharia is Islamic law and as all other religions have their laws, Sharia stands out for several reasons. It is the central obsession of radical Muslims. In other words, every radical Muslim believes it is his or her religious duty to apply Sharia and spread it. There are two sources for Sharia: The Quran and Sunnah; Sunnah is basically Prophet Muhammad's Sayings and Actions. Sharia, according to radical Muslims, has applications in almost all aspects of life such as marriage, war, justice and criminal law, economics, theology and rituals, and generally, all sides of behavior and activities of an individual or a society. The problem with Sharia is that a large portion of its laws is either not practical or draconian. For example, Sharia allows men to marry a child since the prophet Muhammad actually married a child. A husband is given the right to beat up his wife. Criminal laws allow corporal punishment and torture. Moreover, Sharia did not outline any democratic principles. There is no freedom of religion or freedom of expression under Sharia law. There is no freedom of thought or conscience. Any questioning of Allah or the Quran, for example, is considered blasphemous and punishable by death. Yet, the worst part of Sharia is that it is Allah's final word and the prophet's binding tradition and no one should object to them or request any kind of review or amendments even though they are many centuries old. Ironically, Sharia never worked successfully in any Muslim society in the last fifteen centuries of trial and failure. Islamic societies that enjoyed great times of scientific and literary accomplishments were during those spells in Islamic history when radicals were the least influential and rationalism was at its peak. Strangely, some radical Muslims want Sharia to be applied in Western societies today.

Chapter Seventeen

Blasphemy

What is the punishment for blasphemy in a Muslim country? We have seen the rage among Muslims when a cartoonist in France or Denmark draws an image of Muhammad in a way that offends Muslims. How often do we make fun of Moses and Jesus and the Pope and the Bible itself?

While I was teaching a class, a student came in and said that the police are on campus looking for a blogger who was tracked down to our campus. There was suddenly a huge tension felt in the air. I could see that some students had started deleting material on their cell phones and laptops. I knew later that the police could confiscate any electronics suspected in the mentioned incident and definitely some students were complaining that their cell phones were seized by the police. It was all strange to me. I did not know exactly the dimensions of the incident at all. For the next five gruesome days other related events kept unfolding to my shock and to everybody else's as well.

The first thing I learned during those days was that our campus wireless connection was used by a journalist, blogger, activist, and poet named Hamza Kashgary, aged twenty-three years old to tweet some thoughts on the occasion of the birthday of the Muslim prophet Muhammad. I also learned from other sources such as local and international media outlets that the tweets were offensive and considered blasphemous.

So what did that young journalist say? I wept so hard that day when I learned that innocent expression of tender personal ideas could be the cause of one's execution. Kashgary wrote some poetic thoughts addressing the prophet as follows:

"On your birthday, I shall not bow to you. I shall not kiss your hand. Rather, I shall shake it as equals do, and smile at you as you smile at me. I shall speak to you as a friend, no more."

He also added that:

"On your birthday, I find you wherever I turn. I will say that I have loved aspects of you, hated others, and could not understand many more."

Kashgary poetically also tweeted:

"On your birthday, I will say that I have loved the rebel in you, that you've always been a source of inspiration to me, and that I do not like the halos of divinity around you. I shall not pray for you."

As a matter of fact, I find so much beauty and lyricism in those words; there is even plenty of gracefulness and poeticism in them. Moreover, there is a tremendous amount of love and feelings for the prophet Muhammad rather than any offense or blasphemy. But the dark minds could not see any of these beautiful sentiments. They only see hatred and blasphemy which reflects their inner sordidness and ugliness.

***

So what reaction did ensue from the public? A huge surge of calls to kill "blasphemous Hamza Kashgary." Thousands of calls to put Kashgary on trial for apostasy signaled the end for him. Meanwhile, Kashgary managed to slip on a plane headed to Malaysia and landed there few hours later. Upon arrival, the Malaysian authorities arrested him as the Saudi authorities sought immediate extradition of the journalist. An Interpol notice was even issued upon the request of the Saudi authorities.

Few days later, poor Kashgary was handed to a representative of the Saudi authorities and flown back to Riyadh the same day despite Human Rights organizations calls to free Kashgary and Amnesty International pleading with the Malaysian authorities not to proceed with the extradition.

***

These events that started in February 2012 did reveal something important in Saudi society; a chasm in that society that showed more than fifty thousand people had called for his execution. Surprisingly there were more than fifty thousand Saudis who petitioned the King to drop all charges of blasphemy against Kashgary as well. For the first time in Saudi Arabia, there were those who opposed indiscriminate blasphemy charges; this was something that was unheard of in the past. Saudi society has changed. To my surprise, ten of my students told me they were among those who demanded freedom for Kashgary.

The events also revealed that despite Kashgary's pleas with Malaysian authorities and New Zealand authorities to grant him asylum, he was granted none. He was instead whisked into an airplane to Saudi Arabia, into uncertain fate, into sure condemnation, into certain death. I did not hear about him as of August 2012. The fate of this poet and activist is in the dark.

Chapter Eighteen

Sharia and Seductive Eyes

Sharia law is permeating the life of Saudis in every way. The following story, like all stories in this book, sheds light on the social life and the role of Sharia in the lives of Muslims. Looking at the story from a sociological perspective, it outlines some structural and dimensional patterns that shape life in Muslim countries. It is still poignant for me to recount it for the eccentric and quirky content of the story. Like many things in Saudi Arabia and ultra conservative countries, one is likely to be examining an extreme pattern of social life.

In June of 2010, a media report released by Saudi news outlets said that "women in the Kingdom will not be allowed to show their eyes, especially if the eyes are seductive and beautiful." I first thought it was a joke but it turned out to be a true story. What happened was that a member of the religious police, called "Mutawe," saw a woman with her face completely covered as tradition and religious laws demand, but her eyes seemed to him very "seductive."

Religious police is a government department that is responsible for ensuring that all Islamic laws or *Sharia* are observed in public and in private homes, too. Members of the department are given wide judicial powers of arrest, indictment and punishing. A person may be arrested for an indefinite time without trial if the "Mutawe" deems it appropriate or necessary to preserve Islamic laws. Religious police are officially called the "Prevention of Vice and the Promotion of Virtue Authority". The name indicates their loose mission that can be taken or interpreted anywhere and anyway members of the Authority wish at their unquestioned discretion. The members always pride themselves that they are protecting Islam. A big mission!

Hence, a new edict was issued cautioning any woman with tempting or seductive eyes would be arrested immediately. Ironically, women in Saudi Arabia and in other conservative countries are obliged to wear a black covering-all dress called "Abaya." A Saudi woman is literally covered from head to toe and got only two holes in front of her eyes to see through when walking outside her home. However, it seems that someone wanted to even close those two holes as if a woman's seductiveness is that dangerous from those eyes, the tiny holes.

My interpretation is that those members of the religious police either hate women so much or are just afraid of them. Women are often flogged for any act of indecency, or whenever deemed so. Women can be jailed or tortured if thought to be playful in any way. A laugh in public with her husband is forbidden and can land both the husband and wife in jail. A laugh! I am not talking about a kiss in public to her husband. A kiss to a man not related to her is even a serious crime. A heinous crime.

Tradition and Islamic law are supreme in conservative countries. Radicals and terrorists are forcing their women to wear the "Abaya" even when they travel abroad outside their conservative countries. We have seen many women covered in the black "Abaya." Many women have voiced their rejection to this practice of their radical husbands and fathers. Radicals are bent on forcing their extreme brand of Islam while moderate peaceful Muslims, who constitute the majority among Muslims in the West, in Asia, and in Africa reject these practices and always prefer tolerant Islam. If radicals keep pushing for their agenda, the results will be very serious and ominous.

Chapter Nineteen

Chairs and Sins

This is surreal and may be the joke that some readers were waiting for even though it is a real story. There was that religious program on Saudi TV which I liked to watch every now and then to see the state of religion in the Islamic world. The host of the show was a cleric named Al-Habib Umar Ben Muhammad Ben Salem Ben Hafeez.

The subject of that episode was that chairs should not be used to sit on especially by women. First, the cleric started his talk by a long diatribe against the West for introducing chairs into the Islamic world. He emphasized that the West is keen on destroying Muslims and Islam by promoting its inventions that are not in any way conforming to Islamic traditions and values and one of these innovations is the chair. Yes. The chair that we all sit on. Why?

The cleric surprised me when he said that devils would have sex with women when they sit on chairs. "Women become an easy open target for fornication," the cleric Ben Hafeez said.

I was not paying attention to what he was saying full throttle at the beginning of the clerics' speech. I was searching on my laptop for some news about the latest developments in both Libya and Egypt since these two countries were gripped by popular uprisings and civil unrest for a while then. I put the laptop aside and listened to the cleric.

He affirmed that when a woman sits and opens her legs for few seconds, "a devil will presently start to copulate with her." I was in disbelief of what I just heard. The cleric continued to explain that some women confided to him (since he is a trusted preacher and it is normal for anyone to tell him of all sorts of embarrassments and confessions) that they felt orgasms and wet secretions while sitting on chairs at home or outside home.

The cleric then emphasized that the "early great Muslims never used chairs and never sat on one" but rather they always sat on the "ground which reminds humans that they were made from dust and that teaches humans to be humble while a chair would make us vain, conceited, arrogant, pompous, and open to furtive copulation."

I was still in awe and shock while I was writing down all the information he was saying. At the end, the cleric stressed that it is a sin to sit on a chair, especially ones with openings in the seat part where one lays his or her buttocks. "At this point, the devil may take advantage of unwary and unmindful women who are oblivious of the devil's presence." The cleric did not forget to lash out once more at Western inventions and its malicious intentions that try to destroy the sinless Islamic way of life. So this was the state of radicalized Islam as of March 2012. Luckily, the majority of peaceful and moderate Muslims reject those extremes.

Chapter Twenty

Sexual Imagination and Social Repression

A Saudi university professor, named, Doctor Wafaa Al-Sweilam of Al-Imam Islamic University in Riyadh gave a hilarious advice to Muslim women; she advises every Saudi woman (women cover their faces completely in Saudi Arabia) to not walk next to their children if she is good looking and her children are also good looking lest strange men should envisage her face by looking at her children.

This is not a joke though. This is a true story that was circulated in the Saudi papers and all TV land and satellite channels. It was an important advice that was considered the important story and advice of the year for Saudi women who wanted to protect themselves from "depraved" men.

Saudi Arabia is a closed society in the literal sense of the word. Contact between men and women, therefore, is naturally forbidden. Women go to a special section in the bank, for example, to withdraw money or deposit a check. Women enter from a different door. Women are not supposed to look at men; men, unsurprisingly, are not supposed to look at women even though a woman does not show her face at all in public anyway.

This kind of conservative environment evolved into an unhealthy pattern of behavior to the extent that men try to visualize women.

Chapter Twenty-One

Sharia and Legal Infanticide

In early January of 2012, disturbing news reported that a famous Islamic preacher killed his five-year old daughter because he had suspicions she was behaving immorally. The news came from both Saudi sources as well as from abroad. Hospital sources in Riyadh mentioned that the five-year old suffered from signs of torture, immense trauma, burning of large parts of the tiny body, broken limbs, lacerated skin, and a fractured skull.

The father, a renowned powerful TV tycoon and Islamic cleric, said he was "disciplining the girl for her sexually immoral behavior according to Islamic rules of the Quran and the prophet Muhammad sayings." However, after the media uproar inside the Kingdom of Saudi Arabia and abroad, the preacher was arrested and arraigned. The preacher's defense lawyer cited the Quran and prophet's sayings that give a parent the right to discipline a child.

The lawyer even said that the father cannot be prosecuted for murdering a son or daughter according to a religious rule. The lawyer cited the rule from the *Al-Moghny Book* of Islamic law and Sharia by the Muslim scholar Ibn Kodama (b. 1146 - d. 1223 CE):

> *"A father cannot be executed for killing his child while*
>
> *a mother would be for killing her child."*

So based upon this Islamic rule, the father will be able to walk away unscathed. Moreover, when the court day came, the lawyer cited the above source and other sources that allow a father to discipline a child to any degree of punishment to "straighten out the manners of the child." To my shock and to the shock of many, after one month of trial, the father was actually acquitted of all wrongdoing.

The mother was furious before and after the trial. She was in shock to learn about the fate of her daughter. We learned also from the media that she was divorced from the father and he had temporary custody of the girl. The mother described the father as a violent, bad-tempered person who was capable of hiding his true character when he was on TV preaching about Islam and how to be a good pious Muslim. She mentioned that he was very knowledgeable about religion but hardly tried to live up to what he was preaching.

***

As we thought the case was over, the father appeared on one TV show explaining what happened and mentioned that his deceased daughter touched him one time and kissed him. That same night, he dreamt of having sex with his daughter and he could not stand the fact that the daughter touched him that evening and that how he thinks she was a sexual immoral girl and needed to be disciplined.

Learning that, it became obvious to me and to everyone who heard that untold side of the story that the immoral one was the father, the renowned preacher whose perverted unconscious led him to have sex with her in his dream. It is normal for a child to touch her father or look for a hug or a kiss. This is called parental love. It is a natural behavior for a child to seek comfort and safety with a parent. Albeit for that father with his distorted inner mind, it was a crime for the daughter to come near him.

Upon further analysis of the father's violent reaction, it becomes clear that his sexual drive and aggression concurred at the point when he interpreted in his mind that it is the daughter's touching him that is immoral and deserved to be punished. He failed to realize that the little girl behaved naturally and it is his mind that harbors the sexual immorality that is stemming from long inhibitions and social oppression.

At no point the preacher mentioned any behavior that may be deemed off color by the little girl. He kept saying that she touched him and leaned to hug him. He even mentioned that he did not react at that time. He just went around his usual business that evening. When the night came and in the morning he realized he had a dream that involved partial sexual intercourse with his five-year old daughter.

***

The preacher thought in his weak mind that morality entails torturing the child and break her skull in order to purify her of her "sexual immorality." It was him in fact that needed his mind to be purified, not hers. But clearly he blamed her entirely for the whole incident.

The preacher needed also to know that his unconscious was the part of the mind that exposed his true intentions; the intentions that he even could not say to himself. Definitely, his dream reflected a serious complex he had since its content (having sex with his little daughter) manifested a perverted, unnatural desire or behavior. Therefore, the preacher's self-defense mechanism consisted of denial, projection (accusing the little girl of immorality), and rationalization (justifying the brutal punishment that led to his daughter's death).

***

Sadly and ironically, the preacher was back to his TV show preaching people on how to follow Islam and behave in accordance to its principles. People seem to have forgotten what he did because he owns a very powerful weapon, religion. One can brandish that weapon and do everything with it: On can kill, convince, threaten, justify, rationalize, intimidate, hypnotize, scare, allure, mesmerize, charm, defend, validate, defend, substantiate, terrorize, bully, legalize, hide, corroborate, diminish, attenuate, criminalize, decriminalize, conceal, prove, disprove, and authenticate anything he wants or desires.

Chapter Twenty-Two

Egypt and Saudi Arabia Relations:

A History of 1400 Years of Hate and Rivalry

The population of Saudi Arabia was estimated in 2012 by the Saudi government at twenty-seven million people, of whom about eight millions are non-nationals who work as anything from university professors, physicians, taxi drivers to domestic help. The main contingents of foreign nationals are Egyptians, Bangladeshis, Pakistanis, Indians, Syrians, Yemenis, Philippines, Indonesians, and Jordanians and several more other nationalities. However, it is estimated that Egyptians make up the biggest contingent, a little above two millions. They are mainly teachers, physicians, pharmacists, professors, nurses, drivers, hospitality personnel (hotel and restaurant managers, cooks, and waiters), and hand labor. The reason is of course is the proximity of Egypt to Saudi Arabia; Egypt has the best education level in the region, the Arabic language, and the Egyptian Sunni faith which is the same as the Saudis.

Despite the outward harmony between the two peoples of Saudi Arabia and Egypt, there runs deep a huge rift between them. History shows an enormous chasm. Therefore, the Saudi government is always wary of Egyptians working in Saudi Arabia. Among the Egyptians working and living in Saudi Arabia, there is a felt tension that wells up some times in many forms.

Every now and then, we heard of arrests of Egyptians for different reasons, some justified and others that were sort of warning to the rest of the Egyptian colony in Saudi Arabia. There had been a number of highly publicized cases of Egyptian women being arrested and flogged, Egyptian men thrown into jail for extended periods of time with court sentences and without court sentences; there were even reported disappearances of Egyptians who were never found or accounted for.

So what is behind all of this? History has the answer. The Islamic conquest of Egypt took place in 639 CE when the Islamic forces of Omar Ibn Al-Aas under instructions of the second Caliph, Omar Ibn Al-Khattab, invaded Egypt and ended secular Christian Egypt under Roman rule and the Coptic faith domination. The invasion of the whole of Egypt was complete by 641 CE. Many Egyptians were killed as a result, money and gold were plundered, Jizyah (tribute tax) was imposed; food and wheat in large amounts were taken and sent to Medina. The reign of Omar Ibn Al-Khattab and Uthman Ibn Affan, after him, saw great prosperity that had never been seen again in the Islamic state thanks to plundering the riches of Egypt. Poor Egyptians at that time who could not pay the Jizyah because they lost their property or money to the Muslim invaders converted to Islam, but later they changed history when Uthman was killed in 656 CE.

***

So the second historical event that shapes much of the modern-day tense relationship between Egyptians and Saudis and lurks deep in the collective unconscious of the two peoples is the killing of Uthman Ibn Affan in 656 CE. Uthman was accused of favoritism and was killed for that. How and who killed Uthman in Medina? The Muslim ruler of Egypt at the time who was appointed by Uthman was Abdullah Ibn Saad. In early 656 CE, he was deposed by the Egyptians. It was part of an act of revolt against Uthman in Egypt, Basra and Kufa in Iraq. Uthman felt that his rule and life were in danger. It is worth mentioning that it was Uthman who made drastic changes to the Quran original text.

Two months before his killing, Uthman summoned representatives from Egypt, Basra, and Kufa in an attempt to salvage his reign. The representatives were very angry and grew in number, but Uthman could convince them of change. The Basra and Kufa contingents left home, but the Egyptian contingent, now more than a thousand militants strong, laid siege to Uthman's house for forty days in Medina, the capital city of the Muslim state at the time and finally killed Uthman. The Egyptians apparently harbored a lot of anger and resentment against the Islamic rule of Egypt and did not forget the plundering done at the hands of the Islamic invaders years earlier. Moreover, the Egyptian contingent still in Medina, supported Ali Ibn Abi Talib (Uthman's arch enemy who refused to defend Uthman during the siege) to succeed Uthman as the next Muslim Calif.

On the whole, these incidents shape today much of the overwrought relationship between Egypt and Saudi Arabia. The Egyptians will not forget the Arab invasion of their holy land and the Saudis will not forget that the Egyptians killed the Muslim Khalif, Uthman Ibn Affan.

warning to the rest of the Egyptian colony in Saudi Arabia. There had been a number of highly publicized cases of Egyptian women being arrested and flogged, Egyptian men thrown into jail for extended periods of time with court sentences and without court sentences; there were even reported disappearances of Egyptians who were never found or accounted for.

So what is behind all of this? History has the answer. The Islamic conquest of Egypt took place in 639 CE when the Islamic forces of Omar Ibn Al-Aas under instructions of the second Caliph, Omar Ibn Al-Khattab, invaded Egypt and ended secular Christian Egypt under Roman rule and the Coptic faith domination. The invasion of the whole of Egypt was complete by 641 CE. Many Egyptians were killed as a result, money and gold were plundered, Jizyah (tribute tax) was imposed; food and wheat in large amounts were taken and sent to Medina. The reign of Omar Ibn Al-Khattab and Uthman Ibn Affan, after him, saw great prosperity that had never been seen again in the Islamic state thanks to plundering the riches of Egypt. Poor Egyptians at that time who could not pay the Jizyah because they lost their property or money to the Muslim invaders converted to Islam, but later they changed history when Uthman was killed in 656 CE.

***

So the second historical event that shapes much of the modern-day tense relationship between Egyptians and Saudis and lurks deep in the collective unconscious of the two peoples is the killing of Uthman Ibn Affan in 656 CE. Uthman was accused of favoritism and was killed for that. How and who killed Uthman in Medina? The Muslim ruler of Egypt at the time who was appointed by Uthman was Abdullah Ibn Saad. In early 656 CE, he was deposed by the Egyptians. It was part of an act of revolt against Uthman in Egypt, Basra and Kufa in Iraq. Uthman felt that his rule and life were in danger. It is worth mentioning that it was Uthman who made drastic changes to the Quran original text.

Two months before his killing, Uthman summoned representatives from Egypt, Basra, and Kufa in an attempt to salvage his reign. The representatives were very angry and grew in number, but Uthman could convince them of change. The Basra and Kufa contingents left home, but the Egyptian contingent, now more than a thousand militants strong, laid siege to Uthman's house for forty days in Medina, the capital city of the Muslim state at the time and finally killed Uthman. The Egyptians apparently harbored a lot of anger and resentment against the Islamic rule of Egypt and did not forget the plundering done at the hands of the Islamic invaders years earlier. Moreover, the Egyptian contingent still in Medina, supported Ali Ibn Abi Talib (Uthman's arch enemy who refused to defend Uthman during the siege) to succeed Uthman as the next Muslim Calif.

On the whole, these incidents shape today much of the overwrought relationship between Egypt and Saudi Arabia. The Egyptians will not forget the Arab invasion of their holy land and the Saudis will not forget that the Egyptians killed the Muslim Khalif, Uthman Ibn Affan.

***

The third historical incident that affected dramatically the Egyptian-Saudi relationship is at the time of Muhammad Ibn Abdel Wahab (b. 1703 - d. 1792 CE), the founder of the fundamentalist Salafi Islam, known as Wahabism, or Wahabi Islam. Muhammad Ibn Abdel Wahab with another tribesman, named Muhammad Ibn Saud (Great grandfather of the founder of modern-day Saudi Arabia, King Abdul Aziz Ibn Saud and his son kings of today) started to form an Islamic state based on fundamentalist Islam and thus challenging the Ottoman Empire of which Saudi Arabia or Najad and Hejaz as they were called at that time was an integral part.

The new Saudi Wahabi State under Ibn Saud and Abdel Wahab gained initial success and reached far and beyond the borders of Syria and Egypt. In 1818 CE, however, the Egyptian Ruler Muhammad Ali ordered his son, Ibrahim Pasha, to end the Saudi Wahabi State. Ibrahim Pasha destroyed the Saudi capital, Aldareya, and both Najad and Hejaz came under Egyptian rule for a while and then taken back to the Ottoman Empire a little before the death of Muhammad Ali in 1848. Undoubtedly, this historical incident is still deeply engraved in the Saudi unconscious of the ruling Saudi family and the Saudi people. What happened next is equally distressing.

***

In Egypt in 1952, a group of army officers deposed the Egyptian King, Farouk (d. 1965 in exile). King Farouk was a strong ally of the Saudi ruling family. The removal of a royalty in the region sent chills up the backbone to all royalty in the region. The new regime in Egypt declared the republic, and the new president, Gamal Abdel-Nasser, (b.1918 - d. 1970 CE) quickly announced his detestation to all royal regimes as being, according to Nasser, reactionary regimes. Furthermore, Nasser sent forces to the Saudi borders in Yemen and openly supported the revolution against the Yemeni king, who was also a strong ally of the Saudi ruling family. The royal regime in Yemen ended by the help of Egyptian forces in 1962. The relationship between Saudi Arabia and Egypt remained very strained for more than ten years even after Nasser's death in 1970.

The death of Nasser ushered in a new relationship between Saudi Arabia and Egypt. It was payback time. There was another invasion from Saudi Arabia for the second time. The first was, of course, when Omar Ibn Al-Aas invaded Egypt in 639 CE. The second invasion started in the seventies of the twentieth century. It was not a military religious one, like the first one; it was just a religious one.

Wahabism, the radical, extremist strain of Islam, has taken over Saudi Arabia in full by the middle of the nineteenth century. It started to expand outward until it reached Egypt by the seventies of the twentieth century when Egyptian workers started to go to Saudi Arabia seeking work; the Egyptian workers adopted all Wahabi doctrines and transported them back to Egypt. By the year 2000 almost

50% of Egyptians were following the strict Wahabi interpretation of Islam. After the elections of 2012 in Egypt, a Muslim Wahabi fundamentalist president, Muhammad Morsi, became Egypt's first Muslim Brotherhood Wahabi ruler of the land of Egypt; the cradle of civilization finally succumbed to radical Islam. However, secular Egyptians, Egyptian moderate Muslims, Egyptian Christians, liberals, and intellectuals (together, they are 85% of the population) will continue to fight against this fascist takeover of the land of Egypt by radical Muslims till Egypt is liberated.

It is also very crucial to point out that there is a difference in the eyes of Saudis between Wahabism and the Muslim Brotherhood. The Muslim Brotherhood does not see that difference. That is why the Brotherhood will never get any substantial support from the Saudis or the Wahabis. Moreover, The Saudi government was not happy to see a "democratic" Islamic regime thriving in Egypt which would be the attention of Muslim radicals in Saudi Arabia and that might encourage them to emulate in Saudi Arabia.

All these major historical incidents over fourteen centuries have seeped into the collective unconscious of the Saudis and the Egyptians. I had four Egyptian colleagues working in the department where I worked. Many more worked in other departments and colleges. I could feel on a daily basis the nervousness of Egyptians living and working in Saudi Arabia, especially those who are not following the strict radical Wahabi code. Those who are not followers try to fake an allegiance to Wahabism as I was told by many.

So what is Saudi Arabia's strategy? Spreading Wahabism. By spreading Wahabism, Saudis are guaranteed an ideological supremacy. They can then control the environment internally and abroad. In other words, Saudi Arabia got a very powerful weapon whose fear factor is effective. Wahabism simply sets a person to choose between Allah and Muhammad on one hand or eternal damnation in hell, on the other. The result is always a triumph for the pulpit, i.e., the clergy certainly win against secularism in that part of the world.

Can Saudi Arabia and Egypt find themselves in any alliance? Yes, if there is a common enemy threatening them both. It is possible for both countries to band up together if convenience makes it so. It happened several times in the past and will happen again in the future.

However, Saudi Arabia does not accept any ideology from abroad whether it is Western, Egyptian (the Brotherhood is Egyptian) or Iranian. Why Iranian? Iran is one of two arch enemies of the Saudi regime, a topic which will be explored in the next chapter.

Chapter Twenty-Three

Saudi Arabia and Iran

For us in the West, we lump the Islamic world in one bundle. That is a big strategic mistake we often make, even though the U.S. military and the intelligence community such as the CIA, for example, are aware of that, yet Muslims are treated as one body. The differences between the various Islamic nations are huge; they are cultural, nationalistic, linguistic, strategic, doctrinal, ideological, and historical.

Islamic countries such as Indonesia, Mali, Pakistan, Jordan, and Azerbaijan are examples of the extreme differences between Muslim countries where no common language, history, regional interests, economic concerns, strategic plans, cultural components, national aspirations, ideological policies, or doctrinal apparatuses are in any way similar. In fact, they are so far apart that the Islamic component that seemingly unites them actually blurs completely beside these gigantic differences. Moreover, it is significant to state that Islam is the one factor that divides Muslims and leads to their disintegration as there are so many factions, each claiming to be the more pious, more Islamic, and more authentic than the other.

Saudi Arabia and Iran are two more examples of that polarity. They stand diametrically divergent. They speak two different languages (Arabic vs. Persian). They are completely different historically. The peoples' dispositions are widely secluded. They are different culturally. Strategically, Saudi Arabia is completely under constant Western military monitoring and protection for its strategic oil reserves while Iran has been since 1979 a threat to the West and Western interests. One can say that Saudi Arabia is forced to be a Western ally, not by choice, though, for the Saudis. Iran is considered by the West a pariah state, so to speak, but the United States may change strategy and accept Iran as an ally anytime. It is noteworthy to mention that Saudi Arabia's outward alliance with the West is a strategic choice since it is under constant threat from its arch enemy, Iran.

However, the biggest point of departure between The Kingdom of Saudi Arabia and The Islamic Republic of Iran is denominational. Saudi Arabia is mainly a Sunni Muslim country while Iran is Shiah Muslim country. The doctrinal differences lie essentially in the Shiites' belief that Ali was supposed to lead the Muslim state right after Muhammad's death by virtue of Ali's position as Muhammad's son in-law while Sunnis deny that assumption and they further claim that the three first caliphs, Abu Bakr, Omar and Uthman, were rightfully to succeed Muhammad and finally Ali at the end. Shiites, however, feel that Ali was shortchanged and wronged. The division between Sunnis and Shiites is not only about Ali's right of succession, but also goes as far as ritual differences, Islamic practice protocols, interpretation of the Quran, and jurisprudence.

***

There are about two Million Shiites in Saudi Arabia which has a total population of about twenty-seven million people as of 2012, of which there are about eight million non-nationals (basically foreign workers). The Shiite population in Saudi Arabia is mostly concentrated in Al-Shargyia Province, which is the Eastern part of Saudi Arabia i.e., the part which is overlooking the Arab-Persian Gulf that separates Saudi Arabia from Iran. It is also the area in Saudi Arabia mostly rich in oil. The major cities where most Shiites live are Al-Dammam, Al-Jubayl, Al-Hufuf, and Al-Dhahran.

In Iran, there is a considerable Sunni minority of about 10% of the total population (other sources put that percentage at 18% or more). The population of Iran exceeds eighty millions as of 2012. There are no Sunni concentrations in Iran unlike Shiites concentrations in Saudi Arabia which creates a big problem for Saudi authorities to control; Iran, on the other hand, does not have that problem because the Sunnis are evenly dispersed all over the country. The biggest concentration is of fifty thousand Sunnis in Ahwaz, in west Iran near the Arab-Persian Gulf.

Both regimes are brutally cracking down on the Shiites and Sunnis minorities in their respective countries. There have been many political riots and uprisings by both minorities in the last few years from 2005 to 2012. During these years, hundreds of Shiites in Saudi Arabia were arrested, jailed, tortured, and killed. In Iran, hundreds of Sunnis were arrested, jailed, tortured, and killed.

The history of the two nations goes back to 637 CE during the reign of the second Caliph, Omar, when Muslim forces invaded Persia and ended the rule of the Sassanid Empire. Like Egypt, the Iranians feel deep down in their collective unconscious that the Saudis may do it again. On the other hand, the Saudis know there will be payback any time from the Iranians. They know Iran is bigger in population and has aspirations to lead the Islamic world at the expense of Saudi Arabia and its oil. For the Iranians, it is only a matter of time to do this. Therefore, the tension between the two countries is so strong and vibrant that they are edgy over any move or potential change that is likely to happen.

Saudi Arabia's other enemy is Israel. However, the Saudis are more apprehensive of the Iranians than they are of the Israelis. As a matter of fact, Saudi Arabia would ally itself with Israel, despite all the historical, religious, and ideological differences with the Jewish state, rather than finding itself falling under Iranian rule. In Saudi Arabia, there is more outward animosity towards Iran and the Shiites than to Israel and Jews. This does not mean Saudis will kiss and hug Jews any time soon or even ever. For the Saudis, who are very shrewd and competent strategists, it is only a matter of prioritizing battles or staggering wars, so to speak, i.e., one enemy at a time.

Chapter Twenty-Four

Saudi Arabia and Iraq

During the second half of the twentieth century, Saudi Arabia had four enemies, namely, Socialist Egypt of Nasser, Baathi Iraq of Saddam Hussein, The Jewish State of Israel, and The Shiah Islamic Republic of Iran. Nasser and Saddam are dead and their ideologies are long gone. Israel is not an immediate danger. The United States' assurances are enough for now as long as oil keeps flowing to the West and that there are no direct hostilities towards Israel. Iran is being squarely deterred by the West.

Thus why is Iraq a headache for Saudi Arabia? Saddam was a fearful bully of the region till his elimination in 2003, the year of his arrest, and finally in 2006, the year of his execution. Saddam was used well by the West for over three decades to serve a role that he played remarkably and efficiently well, but he also played it amazingly idiotically. When his part was over, he was heard no more after all his strutting and fretting for so long. Saddam filled the world with much sound and fury during his wars against Iran (1981-1989), Kuwait and Coalition forces (1990-1991) and then the rest of the world, namely, the United States and its allies (2003).

Years after the death of Saddam (b. 1937 - d. 2006) and the complete change of regime, Saudi Arabia is still both wary and apprehensive of Iraq. The reason lies in history, fourteen centuries back. During the reign of the Muslim Caliphs Abu Bakr and Omar, Basra and Kufa in Iraq were invaded by Muslim forces (from about 634 to 638 CE) and again the

Iraqis feel deep down in their collective unconscious that they were defeated by the Arabs of Saudi Arabia. Iraqis, like Egyptians and Iranians see themselves as owners of great civilizations that the Arabs of the Peninsula (Saudi Arabia today) never had. It is traumatic for these peoples to fall victim to the Islamic conquest and shrug off their great past and civilizations despite their adoption of Islam. They know they lost to the Bedouins of the Peninsula that had no civilization like theirs. "Saudis are desert nomads," any Iraqi, Iranian, or Egyptian would tell each other resenting how Saudis could conquer them and ruin their civilizations.

During the rule of Saddam (1979 - 2003) Sunnis had the upper hand in running Iraq. Iraq has about 60% of its population Shiites. The population of Iraq is about thirty-one millions as of 2012. When the regime changed in 2003, the Shiites came to power to the chagrin of the Saudis and the joy of the Iranians.

Although Iraq is in no position at all to wage any war against any other country for a long time to come, the Saudis are fearful of the future. The Iraqi Shiites voiced their hostility against the Saudis for their role in destroying their country and bombing the Shiite cities during the Kuwait war of 1990-1991.

Moreover, Iraq is a budding democracy under the auspices of the United States. Democracy is an annoying concept lest the Shiites in Saudi Arabia should demand something of it. A Shiite leader in Saudi Arabia said if "the Shiite group in Iraq that had been oppressed under Saddam for so long had finally been liberated, then it can happen here in Saudi Arabia one day."

Saudis are not taking any chances. Iran is watching the scene and waiting. It is in the best interests of Iran to expand Shiah presence outside Iran. Iranians and Iraqis have already shown their intentions when they supported the Shiites of Bahrain (a small country right on the eastern border of Saudi Arabia) during the years of 2011and 2012 Shiah uprisings. Although the uprisings were severely crushed by Bahraini and Saudi forces, the Shiites are waiting for another chance.

All this explains why the Saudis are always nervous at any Iraqi move in the region. One Saudi writer said that "Saddam was just one small devil, and he was Sunni; we wonder what the Shiah devils are having for us and they are so many and so enormous and so ravenous and worst of all, they are in power now in Iraq and have all the support of the Iranians as well which was not even the case when Saddam was in power." So what is Saudi Arabia's plan? Saudi Arabia is working with other powers in the region, namely Turkey, and the West to form a Sunni army mostly of Al-Qaeda fighters, Jihadists, and Wahabis to control Iraq and Syria (whose president Assad is Shiite). The army will be called the Islamic State in Iraq and the Levant, ISIL or ISIS, for short. ISIL may even declare a new Islamic Caliphate. This move by the Saudis and Turks is dangerous and may seriously destabilize the whole region and the world. Turkey's secret plan is to hijack the Caliphate once it is up and running. On the whole, forming ISIL may backfire and hurt the Saudis and the West, but this shows how myopic the West and the Saudis are in dealing with serious issues.

Chapter Twenty-Five

Saudi Arabia and the West

The Islamic Caliphate fell by the defeat of the Ottoman Empire when World War I ended in 1918. The Caliphate was officially ended by the secular Turkish leader Kemel Ataturk in 1924. When the British thought of the oil and Mecca, the center of Islam, they could not find someone better than King Abdul Aziz Ibn Saud as the leader of the vast area of what we know today as Saudi Arabia. And he was the best choice and his sons proved even better.

King Abdul Aziz Ibn Saud came to power when he was granted Saudi Arabia under two conditions:

1- Oil will keep flowing to the West without any conditions and at market price.

2- No return to Islamic Caliphate at any price.

In return, the West will turn its back and ignore completely all human rights abuses taking place in Saudi Arabia. Deal!

The world understands the war for oil, but what about the Caliphate? The fall of the Caliphate was a good sign that Islam was ebbing in the world and the Saudi king had to work hard for that goal. How could the family of the rulers of Saudi Arabia manage to rule the center of Islam without the Caliphate?

Simple! By being more Islamic and radical than any Caliphate that ever happened in Islamic history. The Saudi government implemented a number of measures such as establishing the religious police authority, ban on women driving, application of extreme Islamic laws, etc. which guaranteed that Islam in Saudi Arabia would look very rigid, radical, and extremely fundamentalist, so no one would seem more Islamic than the Saudi government or the Saudi people. They all succeeded in achieving that goal and the Saudi rulers passed with red colors and the West could not hide its approval and praise for the Saudis.

The downside was that, unfortunately, another extremely violent brand of Islam sprang up and tried in numerous occasions to highjack the government in Saudi Arabia to establish what they consider true Islamic rule and Caliphate. All attempts so far have failed and brutally crushed. Those violent movements fleshed out later in the form of terrorist groups such as Al-Qaeda led by Osama Bin Laden (a Saudi millionaire himself).

Despite the Saudi government attempts to absorb and contain the Islamic fervor and religious energy of the Saudis and channel them to the benefit of the government, there are some groups that are running out of control now. The West, namely the United States and The United Kingdom took notice and understand the risks. On the other hand, the Saudis are using this to their benefit still by using excessive religious sentiments and fervor to spread Wahabi Islam (the Saudi brand of radical Islam) as their own ideology to control other countries around the Middle East and beyond. Although this is a violation of the deal, one might wonder why the West is tolerating the use of the Saudi Wahabi ideology to take the rest of the world. The answer is simple: The West is not realizing the danger of Wahabism at all. The Saudis are smarter than anyone in the world. Besides, they own a very strong weapon: The Wahabi ideology with which they are already invading the whole world.

Chapter Twenty-Six

A Wife Murder and a Robert Browning Poem

Honor killing is a practice that pestered the world at all times. In the past, we read and heard of men killing their wives for the suspicion of infidelity. In many countries such as the United States and Mexico, we heard of such stories; we often heard of stories how Spanish men would drag their wives by horses till death. In Italy, folklore tales are full of such horrendous stories of jealous men tormented by their wives' unfaithfulness. But that was mainly in the past. Does it happen now? A fairly great deal of such incidents may come up, but not as it used to be.

In Arab and Muslim countries, the law gives the right to a husband to kill the wife and even her lover if caught red-handed i.e., *in flagrante delicto* or simply caught in the act. While this practice is illegal in Western countries (judges may still regard it as an attenuating circumstance in a murder case of a wife), it is still common in Muslim countries. I would like to affirm that it is a cultural practice rather than a religious commandment.

The Latin term *in flagrante delicto* is basically referring to the offence of what might be termed "in the midst of sexual activity." As a matter of fact, in a Muslim country, a husband is sure to walk free if he can prove that he caught his wife in a sexual act at the time of the murder. The penal code in most Muslim countries allows this, and that is why honor killing is still a common practice in many Muslim countries. I reiterate: this is a cultural practice rather than a religious commandment.

In 2010 there was a highly publicized story of a high ranking official, never named and believed to be a member of the Saudi cabinet. Saudi news outlets never reported the incident, but it was reported in other media outlets in Egypt, India, and Lebanon. Thanks to satellite TV channels, one could watch the whole Arab and many Muslim countries media if one lives in one of these countries. And it is all free. Just installing a dish which may cost about eighty dollars, one can get free service from about nine-hundred TV channels from all parts of the Arab and Muslim countries. I availed myself a great deal of this service and I learned a lot.

***

So in addition to hearing the scandal from the non-Saudi media, I heard students in one class talking about a dead body of a half-naked woman being found in the Al-Olaya area, an upscale neighborhood in Riyadh. The woman, they explained, was the wife of a prince or some official in the government. When I inquired about who killed her and why, they giggled and looked at each other. I asked if it was an honor killing. They all seemed to agree. When I asked if she deserves what happened to her, they all seemed to agree, too.

A week later, we read in class a superb poem by Robert Browning titled "My Last Duchess." The poem is simply about a Duke living in the late Italian renaissance named the Duke of Ferrara who was showing a guest of his a painting of his departed wife, a young, beautiful woman who died mysteriously. In the poem, I stopped at few lines and tried to make my students feel for the dead Duchess (and perhaps for the dead woman on the streets of Riyadh).

I read the following lines:

> "She had
> A heart—how shall I say?—too soon made glad,
> Too easily impressed; she liked whate'er
> She looked on;"

I pointed out the simplicity of the dead Duchess and her pure nature. After the students read and understood the lines before and after that part, they were convinced she did nothing wrong. Then I introduced the following lines:

> "She thanked men,—good! But thanked
> Somehow—I know not how—as if she ranked
> My gift of a nine-hundred-years-old name
> With anybody's gift."

I then explained the Duke's arrogance and egocentrism manifested by his bragging about his family name while failing to see his wife's genuine kindness and beauty, instead he saw only unfaithfulness and treachery.

As part of the discussion, I asked the students if there was any reference in the poem of the Duchess' committing any act of betrayal to her husband or any hint of that. They said no. I then asked why then he killed her. Replies included words such as "his paranoia", "egocentrism", and "lack of judgment to appreciate a good wife." I was so happy to hear all that from the students. They got very enthusiastic and became truly involved in the poem which seemed strange to them at the beginning.

The climax in the poem comes in the lines where the Duke decides to, implicitly, get rid of his wife:

> "Oh sir, she smiled, no doubt,
> Whene'er I passed her; but who passed without
> Much the same smile? This grew; I gave commands;
> Then all smiles stopped together. There she stands
>
> As if alive."

The Duke's jealousy is rampant, I explained. He would not accept her to smile to others as a courteous gesture. That drives him mad. He is so selfish, paranoid, and without any measure of self-confidence. Moreover, he stopped her smiles forever because he could not cope with her beautiful, humble nature against his brutal, arrogant disposition. Instead, he had her painting standing only for him to watch and only there he feels so secure.

I could see a lot of change in the eyes of my students. They had no chance to enjoy literature before. It is looked down upon in Saudi Arabia. The Quran is the only text to be read. As a matter of fact, the Quran considers poets heretics and infidels since they distract people from the word of Allah.

Chapter Twenty-Seven

The Arab Spring, (Or Is It?)

One of the darkest episodes of my stay in Saudi Arabia was the Arabic Spring. It was a series of popular uprisings that swept many nations in the Middle East. The uprisings were mainly against several corrupt dictators who stayed in power for so long in several Arabic countries. The uprisings led to change of leadership of those dictators in Tunisia, Egypt, Libya, and Yemen. Although the peoples of those countries had legitimate reasons to rise up against their dictators, the winners at the end were not the legitimate revolutionaries who rose against the dictators, but rather a clique of extremist religious power-thirsty opportunists who usurped leadership from the people and enjoyed absolute despotism in the name of religion.

On the other hand, Saudi authorities feared the uprisings might extend to their territories. For me as an American working in Saudi Arabia, the results were not good at all. Authorities regarded every foreigner as a potential instigator against the rulers of the kingdom. The early assumption when the Arabic Spring started in December of 2010 and then January of 2011, most observers in the Middle East thought it was all the work and agenda of the West. Later development proved otherwise. However, it took the authorities here in Saudi Arabia too long to realize this fact that the West had nothing to do with the uprisings, and that, we the foreigners, were not up to foster similar uprisings in the Gulf region. It was not before things were already made very hard for us, the foreigners. We were under constant watch, our homes and offices were bugged, emails and phones came under surveillance, and every step was counted.

In Egypt in particular, the Muslim Brotherhood won every election and by July 2012, their candidate, Mohammed Morsi, became president of Egypt. The worst thing the Muslim Brotherhood did to Islam was that it helped form an alliance with other radical Islamic factions at the beginning. The Brotherhood and many other groups, such as the Islamic Group (Al-Gamaa Al-Islamiya) and the Fundamentalist Group (Al-Gamaa As-Salafiya) among many other smaller groups, that operated underground for so long for their terrorist agenda, seemed to win all elections even though they did not participate in the uprisings. They all came out thirsty for power and wealth which proves that they are not true spiritual religious groups but rather dishonest opportunists who just love money and power. They showed a lot of animosity against one another later; each accusing the other of trying to usurp power. They, however, succeeded to achieve one goal: the disintegration of the modern state of Egypt.

Chapter Twenty-Eight

A Flood Disaster: A Testimony of Islamic Faith

Around the Hajj time of 2009, we heard of many odd news and we read of numerous incidents that took place around the kingdom. There were flash floods near Mecca where twenty-five people were drowned as a result. The uproar was so far reaching that "many officials in the government were put on trial for failing to predict the floods (predict? That was funny) and take appropriate measures to avoid them." That was the transparency level of Saudi justice: putting officials on trial for failing to predict natural disasters. If the charge affidavit in the arraignment stated that the officials failed to take necessary measures to avoid potential danger or possible disasters, things would have been different from a logical and a legal point of view. But "predict?" I was stunned for a long time.

"How can you predict a flash flood?" I asked a Saudi colleague while pretending to be ignorant and implying that one can actually predict a flash flood, so I looked at him waiting for an answer.

"A true Muslim can tell if a disaster is going to happen or not," he replied with an air of confident piety.

"Oh, I see."

"When your heart is full of faith in Allah, you can know everything," he affirmed with certainty.

"How can an official have his heart full of faith, which is something good, you know, and predict things at the same time?" I said hiding my sarcasm and sounding like I really wanted to know.

***

"First, a person has to follow Sharia and apply all Quran and all the Prophet's, Peace be upon him, teachings in his life and then the person will have no problem and never gets into trouble," he affirmed with an apparent large deal of smugness and self-confidence.

"Has any one with such great faith in Allah and the prophet ever got into trouble of any sort?" I asked with tongue in cheek. I was really upset, but I could not show any outward signs of being fed up with their smugness in their faith.

"No."

"Not any one?"

"It depends on how faithful they are; I mean the degree of their faith," he explained.

"You mean those officials who are in jail now and those who died as a result of the floods were really unfaithful or perhaps infidels, I guess," I said quietly and slowly.

"I don't know for sure; only Allah and the prophet (Prayers be upon him) know," he said in a confused way.

"But you said faithful people don't get into trouble while unfaithful people do get into trouble and clearly some died and others were sent to jail," I explained.

"Yes, they must be unfaithful then," he quickly concluded.

"Didn't you say only Allah and the prophet know?" I asked trying to sound naive.

"Prayers be upon him," he added. "Yes, I said that," he said. Clearly, he was contradicting himself and he was aware of it.

I noticed also every time the word "prophet" or "Muhammad" is mentioned, one must say "prayers be upon him."

***

The following day, I cautiously approached my Saudi colleague and without opening that particular subject again, I gingerly brought in the idea of logical fallacies. I say "gingerly" because I had no idea whether he knew about logical fallacies altogether.

"Dr. Mahmoud, how are you today?"

"Al-Hamdu lillah," he answered contently. Thanking Allah is always the answer to any greeting in Islamic societies.

"Have you heard of logical fallacies, Dr. Mahmoud? Do you know what they mean?" I asked. All night and morning, I was so upset and I was determined to talk to him about making wrong conclusions without proof.

"What is that?"

So I explained logical fallacies generally; then I specifically elaborated on one particular fallacy that pertains to the subject of whether faithful people are saved while infidels are not. I introduced "Affirming the Consequent Fallacy." I explained that:

1- If there is X, then there is Y.

2- There is Y.

3- Therefore, there is X.

I told him an argument of this sequence is invalid. The conclusion can be false even when statements 1 and 2 are true. Since *X* was never asserted as the *only* sufficient condition for *Y*, other factors could account for *Y* (in case X was false).

I explained to him the following example:

1- If we *assume* that the Dean owns Al-Riyadh Bank (X), then he is rich (Y).

2- The Dean is rich (Y).

3- Therefore, the Dean *actually* owns Al-Riyadh Bank (X).

In 3, the statement is likely to be false because statement 1 or "X" has never been verified or proven at all times to be true; and even if it is true, the Dean can be rich because of other factors.

"Can you see, Dr. Mahmoud, that one can be harmed for many reasons, not just because one is faithful or an infidel?"

He looked at me in a smirk and said "I have a class now but we will talk later, maybe tomorrow."

I was not sure what he was up to afterwards.

***

At that time, I was preoccupied with whether my students in the literature class had read *Adventures of Huckleberry Finn*. It was mid semester and I was preparing for lots of tasks such as midterm exams and evaluations and making sure textbooks were available at the bookstore. I knew I was going to analyze a famous part in this novel where there is a conversation between Jim and Huck about speaking a foreign language. It is a funny episode. Huck tells Jim that people in France do not speak English, but rather they speak French. It gets ridiculous when Huck tries to convince skeptical Jim by pointing out that cats and cows do not "talk" in the same way, and that, by analogy, neither should French people and American people.

I also tried sarcastically to plead ignorance and sound naive at times to my Saudi colleague who insists that if one is faithful, he will be saved from all harm, and emphasizing that the unfaithful will definitely be harmed. I could see my Saudi colleague was by far less aware of reality and what actually happens to people in real life.

The following day, I saw Dr. Mahmoud in the office and we started talking about midterm exams and other issues. Then I went back to the subject of the faithful being protected from harm by Allah whereas the unfaithful and the infidels are not spared at all and even if one seems faithful and is harmed, then it is a sign that he or she was not a good faithful person.

***

"So my last point was whether good faithful people ever get hurt. Can a faithful person be harmed?" I said to him. I was really upset and restraining my thoughts.

He said "Sometimes."

I nodded waiting for more concession from him.

"Yes, sometimes," he said and looked away through the window whenever he was pensive. "Yes, anyone can be harmed regardless of who he is," he added to my relief.

"That also means one should not take as true a premise or an assumption that has not been proven to be correct or that has not been validated. Right?" I said softly.

"I think so now," he said looking at me.

He was realizing at that time that disasters can befall anyone regardless of whether one is "a good faithful Muslim or not." I sighed with relief and gave him a smile of encouragement and appreciation. Clearly, introducing to him logical fallacies and discussing them helped him think differently.

I did not feel wasting time or words talking to my Saudi colleague; I knew he would think a little differently from the way he used to before. At least, he might rethink of what he was told or took for granted in his Islamic religion. Islam inspires a huge sense of protection and confidence, but facts and reality indicate that no one, Muslim or non-Muslim, is immune from harm or granted comprehensive protection from Allah.

Chapter Twenty-Nine

Adventures of Huckleberry Finn

Two days later, I started teaching *Adventures of Huckleberry Finn*. It was the second novel in the semester and I was very excited to teach such a funny and marvelous work of art.

It took a short introduction to give the political and social background to Mark Twain's jabs at his society of that time, and it took me a bit longer to explain the language issues of spelling and pronunciation of the characters of the novel. In the following four classes, we delved into the text itself. Of course, I was not going to skip that part where Jim and Huck argue about how French people speak a language different from English. So I read the following part explaining whatever stopped my students' comprehension or enjoyment:

"Why, Huck, doan' de French people talk de same way we does?"

"No, Jim; you couldn't understand a word they said—not a single word."

"Well, now, I be ding-busted! How do dat come?"

"I don't know; but it's so. I got some of their jabber out of a book. S'pose a man was to come to you and say Polly-voo-franzy—what would you think?"

"I wouldn' think nuff'n; I'd take en bust him over de head—dat is, if he warn't white. I wouldn't 'low no nigger to call me dat."

"Shucks, it ain't calling you anything. It's only saying, do you know how to talk French?"

"Well, den, why couldn't he say it?"

"Why, he is a-saying it. That's a Frenchman's way of saying it."

"Well, it's a blame ridicklous way, en I doan' want to hear no mo' 'bout it. Dey ain' no sense in it."

"Looky here, Jim; does a cat talk like we do?"

"No, a cat don't."

"Well, does a cow?"

"No, a cow don't, nuther."

"Does a cat talk like a cow, or a cow talk like a cat?"

"No, dey don't."

"It's natural and right for 'em to talk different from each other, ain't it?"

"Course."

"And ain't it natural and right for a cat and a cow to talk different from us?"

"Why, mos' sholy it is."

"Well, then, why ain't it natural and right for a Frenchman to talk different from us? You answer me that."

"Is a cat a man, Huck?"

"No."

"Well, den, dey ain't no sense in a cat talkin' like a man. Is a cow a man?—er is a cow a cat?"

"No, she ain't either of them."

"Well, den, she ain't got no business to talk like either one er the yuther of 'em. Is a Frenchman a man?"

"Yes."

***

Of course we laughed a lot at the conversation as I acted out much of it; then, I asked the students the following question:

"Where is Huck's mistake in that argument?"

One student said "He should have used parrots or monkeys instead of cats and cows."

"Maybe. It sounds like a funny idea; it never occurred to me, Abdallah; you are funny, Abdallah, but I'm looking for another mistake he did that made the analogy unfeasible. Anyone?" I asked.

Another student suggested "They should have mentioned another language like Spanish."

I laughed and said "No." I stopped and scanned the class for more replies and then said "Look! Here is the answer: It's the use of the analogy between humans and animals that makes it difficult for Huck and Jim to solve the argument or get anywhere. One should not compare two things from different categories, otherwise one makes a logical fallacy called *False Analogy*; it is when one assumes all different categories are similar. You see the mistake that one can make easily?"

I explained this in more details and gave more examples till I felt they got a hang of it. "It is like saying I prefer eating mangoes to playing tennis; two different activities from different categories. You would compare mangoes to oranges and tennis to golf, for example," I elaborated.

Few moments passed and I pretended to be looking for something in the book giving them time to process what I said then added:

"Do you think the writer, Mark Twain, did that intentionally?" I did not wait long for an answer. One student said "Sure, he had a point in mind." I quickly agreed "That this was done intentionally, so we, the readers, would think of what was wrong in our human thinking and reasoning. We mix things and believe in social traditions or what seems as religious truths that are shoved down our throats, but we need to reconsider our beliefs exactly as the American society of that time in the nineteenth century needed to rethink about slavery and many other issues of their time such as treating man as an animal such as a cow." There was a pause and then I looked inside the book and after few seconds I continued:

"So I want you to think every time you make generalizations about anything. Nothing should be taken for granted," I said. Suddenly, I saw the dean walking across the hallway, but I believed that had nothing to do with the class underway. It was a coincidence, I thought.

I then asked "Can you compare your Islamic values to Christian or Jewish values and condemn them because they do not agree with your Islamic values?

"No."

It was a short answer that came from two sides of the class, but I felt I achieved great success that day.

I was not sure if the dean was still outside, but I could see the students' brains working for the first time.

Chapter Thirty

Logical Fallacies and Dogmatic Islamic Theology

To my surprise, in the following class, a considerable number of students asked for more information about logical fallacies. Some understood the meaning behind logical fallacies while others had a relatively small measure than I hoped, so I tried to be as simple as possible and as funny as I could in the new class.

I asked one of the students "Are there any monsters or dragons in the city of Riyadh?"

"No," he laughed.

I asked another student the same question and the answer was also the same.

"Do you know why?" I asked another student.

"I don't know," he said timidly.

I said "Because I bought this watch that I'm wearing and it cost me a million dollars. It has the power to scare away all monsters and dragons."

They laughed. Some stared at me for few moments and then stared at the watch and then laughed. I added "This is a very good practical watch that, though expensive, has a magical power to send any monsters or dragons away," I said with much emphasis.

They laughed and looked at me and then at the watch with uncertainty.

I said "That is right; there are no monsters or dragons in Riyadh thanks to my watch."

"This watch? No way," one student protested.

"Well, I have the proof, my magical watch, and to prove it more: there are not monsters or dragons."

I then explained "This is just a logical fallacy called *proof by lack of evidence* or simply *negative evidence*."

I explained that this was a false argument where one gets to a conclusion or a result only because there is no evidence to counter the conclusion or prove the opposite and because one cannot prove if that watch can actually scare monsters and dragons; it is because there are not any dragons around to put the watch to the test and I used the absence of those creatures (if they exist at all) to prove falsely my point that they had been scared away by this watch.

They laughed and I seized on this and started asking them for similar situations where they or someone they knew would use this type of false argument to their benefit.

After a long pause and after a lot of enticing, one student asked "How?"

***

I said "Tell me please a situation where you make a statement or someone makes a statement which seems correct but in fact it's not; it is just false because of faulty reasoning, simply because you cannot prove the opposite like the example I gave you earlier."

One student mentioned that his radical cleric in his hometown of Mecca used to scare them in the mosque by telling them that there were spirits and ghosts that helped him to know people's secrets and whether they read the Quran daily or not; and whenever the student asked him to tell some of those secrets or show him the ghosts, the cleric just said he would not because they are secrets and the ghosts do not like to come out to ordinary people and he would keep those secrets to himself only.

That was excellent and I did not even expect it.

The student added that "Now I understand why that cleric kept everyone afraid and under control because he always claimed to have that power which could not be proven or disproven at all."

I was impressed at their revelation and their new realizations.

"OK, how about this funny example. If someone says that he drank whisky with some ice and he got drunk two weeks ago; then he says that he drank tequila with some ice and he got drunk last week, and then last night he drank gin with some ice and also he got drunk; then one can conclude that ice, being the common denominator in all those occasions as the cause that makes one drunk. Is that a correct conclusion?"

They all said in one voice "No."

"Exactly! We have to look behind common denominators and there is always the truth; it's the liquor, not the ice."

"We should not be deceived by anyone's deceptive talk," I concluded.

I was so happy to make them think differently and hoped they would continue to do so.

Chapter Thirty-One

The State of Freedom in Saudi Arabia

In a word, the state of freedom in the Kingdom Of Saudi Arabia is "dire." According to Amnesty International report released in 2010, it described the conditions there as terrible for any level of freedom of expression or human rights. The report used among many other epithets to characterize the conditions as "horrific and unimaginable." As a matter of fact, laws that are passed to stem any possibility of popular questioning of the ruling family are draconian and abusive.

Saudi authorities would launch every now and then a wave of repressive and oppressive measures, and it is all in the name of "security and safety of Saudi citizens." That is how the Saudi Ministry of the Interior spokesman would open his statement when he introduces a new package of restrictive decrees.

Amnesty International even said that the new anti-terror laws in Saudi Arabia would treat the least acts of political expression or peaceful dissent as an act of terrorism. While I was there, I witnessed strange events. There were many legal cases where regular Saudi and foreign citizens were prosecuted as terrorists for surfing the internet or chatting casually with undercover agents or unscrupulous informants about social issues or political changes in the region or countries adjacent to Saudi Arabia.

Saudi law allowed authorities to detain "suspects" indefinitely and without trial. The sole intention of the authorities was repression and the spread of fear amongst citizens and foreigners alike. Amnesty International was critical of Saudi repressive laws. It was particularly critical of the kingdom's "vague and broad" definitions of terrorism which could be ranging from "destabilizing society" to "harming the reputation of the state" and everything in between.

It was clear to political observers, watch dogs, and human rights advocates that the Saudi intention was to deter any sort of dissent and the protection of the regime. Therefore, any peaceful meeting or academic discussion that would invoke the least criticism of the state would be labeled right away as "terrorist."

***

Saudi Arabia does not have a constitution or a written penal code as we know it in the West. What they have in Saudi Arabia is a criminal code based on Sharia law or Islamic law, totally uncodified, and loose enough to be interpreted differently by each judge.

Saudi Arabia does not admit having such a thing as political prisoners or prisoners of conscience. They claim they only have criminals and terrorists in their jails. They do not admit having detention centers or concentration camps but only correctional institutions. Although others would see otherwise, yet Saudi authorities never admitted wrongdoing. Torture in the form of beating, hanging from the ceiling by the ankles, sleep deprivation and all other sorts of physical and psychological abuse were common. It was also common that detainees be held for very long periods without trial or access to a legal consultation, and consequently confessions were extracted under such duress.

It was in that climate that I lived and worked, taught and did research. I understood that all countries including Western democracies had their fears of terrorism and had their laws that were vague and broad, but in the West they were aimed at stemming terrorism, not social reform and change. No laws in the West were so draconian and intrinsically abusive as those of Saudi Arabia.

Chapter Thirty-Two

Travelling with Two Wives

Saudi Arabia is the top country in the world in sending students abroad to study. There is a program implemented by the Saudi Ministry of Education that supervises the Saudi educational missions abroad. The United States, Great Britain, Australia, France are top destinations. However, American universities received more Saudi students than any other country.

The many Saudi graduates from American universities that I met in Saudi Arabia had mixed views about life in the United States. They were mostly negative; they often talk about the non-religious life of Americans. They say that Americans do not have morals because American society allows dating. They often criticized what they consider the loose freedom of American life and the absence of Islamic values in America.

Despite the hypocrisy of some of those Saudis I met and their talk of relations they had with American girls and women during their college years, I noticed that most Saudis who graduated from American universities yearn to their life in the United States. They somehow let out their sentimental emotions that express admiration of democracy, political transparency, freedom of expression, the responsibility of officials, the rule of law, the cleanliness of the streets, the organized way of life, citizens' respect of the law, etc. These are some of what third world countries do not have at all even though we in the West do not see them as perfect, yet they are perfect for third world countries' citizens who do not see these in their countries.

One day in October of 2011, one of the Saudi teaching assistants working in our department received a letter from the university administration telling him that he had been nominated for a five-year scholarship to finish his master's and doctorate in language teaching methodology. He was so jubilant and so thrilled that he forgot to take the letter and left it on the desk when he left for home. Without the letter, he would not be able to start the red-tape process to get an exit visa and bank funding. Luckily, early the following morning when he came searching for it, he found it in the trash bin in good shape.

***

Few weeks passed and he called me up at home which was unusual. He talked to me about an uncomfortable situation he wanted my opinion about. He said that he is married to two wives and he did not know if he could take both to the United States. I did not know what advice I should give him, so I told him to wait till the following morning and I might be able to give him a better view of the situation. I had no clue at the time about any solution, but I knew he could not take both wives.

When I saw him the day after, I explained to him that polygamy is illegal in the United States. He said that "one could have several girlfriends."

"That's true theoretically but I don't think you can handle all of them simultaneously," I joked to get him out of his tense mood.

"So what's the difference between girlfriends and wives?" he said intensely and defiantly.

"The marriage contract," I said. "It is illegal to be married to two wives and one would be thrown in jail for polygamy if you have two valid marriage contracts at the same time, but you don't have that contract when you date one or more. Got it?" I said in a neutral manner even though I wanted to laugh at not knowing such simple matter.

"Is there a way I can take both wives with me?" he said in despair.

"Yes, divorce one and take her as the babysitter but I think deciding which one will accept this solution would be a bit of a hassle when you go home today," I said in a very sarcastic way. He did not notice my sarcasm though.

He then said to my surprise "That seems like a possible... actually a good solution." I was mum for a moment. I then asked "Have you tried to see how other colleagues who were in your situation dealt with this issue?"

"I called a colleague who came back from the United States last month and he said he alternated one wife each year."

"I don't understand; what do you mean by 'alternate'?" I really could understand what he meant, but I needed more time to work out the legality and feasibility of that solution.

"It means taking only one wife at a time. One wife each year, but in my case, I love both and I want both with me at the same time; I need both," he pleaded in a manner that showed a man who is inseparable from his two wives. I was about to laugh again.

"What are the regulations of the Saudi Ministry of Education and the university?" I asked hoping that regulations will decide instead of him.

***

It took him one week before he got some news from officials in the Ministry of Education.

"I can take both as long as one is the babysitter," he said jubilantly.

"Was it hard for you *and them* to figure out who would be the babysitter?" I responded with some palpable vexation.

"Yes, there was no problem. They would alternate," he said. At that moment I laughed till tears started rolling from my eyes.

Three days later I was paid an unusual visit at about 1:00 am. The phone was ringing and there was a loud knock on the door, both at the same time. It was scary. When I opened the door, I found my Saudi colleague at the door and apologized for the bizarre visit. In my four years of my residence in Saudi Arabia, I was visited only once by a Saudi and that was the one time visit.

"Can we talk?" he hesitated and stuttered.

"Please come in and what's the matter?" I said, still confounded. I really needed to sleep.

"Are you going to tell anyone about this?" he stuttered again.

"This what?"

"Taking my two wives to America. I can go to jail if they find out."

"I'm not going to talk about anything regarding you, and you said you would divorce one wife, so what's the problem?"

"I cannot divorce anyone. I love both and it is hard you know."

"Look, this is your life and I have no intention to mention this story to anyone, here or in the United States because it is not my business and I have nothing to do with your business. Please rest assured you can handle this your way, OK?" I said with all the strength I had to make him least worried about me.

***

It turned out that another colleague from Syria insinuated to him that I might try to hurt him by reporting him to the American authorities. That Syrian instructor also told him that I might be a spy "as all Americans are spies."

The Saudi colleague kept calling me on the phone every now and then to make sure I was still friendly and I had no ill-intentions. I learned that he travelled few weeks later and

I had no idea to what state or university he went to or how many wives he had in his company and in what capacity one or both were.

Chapter Thirty-Three

Car Drifting and Saudi Politics

In the United States of America, a circuit court judge will tell one that driving is a privilege that can be taken away; not the case in Saudi Arabia. As a matter of fact, it is a right that can be even taken to extreme. This sounds crazy to readers but I had been confounded by what I saw and heard. Driving with no rules of maximum speed limit or lane changing etiquette are some of the freedoms that Saudis have without any restraint.

One day after a class, Ziad (he was a brilliant student who always showed interest about Lady Gaga of whom I knew very little!) approached me and asked me to accompany him and others to a car race.

"A car race? In Saudi Arabia?" I laughed.

"It's a kind of race you will like Mr. Sam. You will see lots of cars and lots of people. Please come," he insisted.

"OK, but when does it start?" I asked.

"Every Wednesday after Aser Prayer (afternoon prayer around 3:00 pm) near *Al-Saha Al-Shargiyyia* (Eastern Plaza)," he said.

"Sure, I'll see you there soon then," I said hurriedly because I needed to grab lunch or any snack.

Saudi weekend starts Wednesday afternoon. Their days off of the week are Thursday and Friday (by June 2013, the Saudi government plans to have the weekend on Friday and

Saturday). It is a little weird for us in the West, but definitely we also know in the West that the Sabbath for Muslims is Friday. Saudis came to appreciate and value their weekends and use them to have fun, but I was not sure how my students and all young people in Saudi Arabia could have quality time during their weekends. It was that day and through the early evening that I learned about the favorite pastime of young people. It was hilarious, shocking, and eye-popping.

***

When I arrived to the area, it was so crowded, hundreds of cars and thousands of young men, reminiscent of Monday football near any stadium in any American city. Thousands of young men; I say young men, not a single woman was there in those events. Fun is only for men, it is noteworthy to point out.

I looked for anyone I knew, but tough. Besides the noise and crowd, there was dust rising a hundred feet in the air. When I arrived and parked my car, I heard loud engines' revving, tires' squealing and young men's loud cheers. Yes, it was car drifting. Car drifting in a public street closed off to any sort of traffic. Sometimes car drifting just takes place on the highway and on city streets with regular drivers and pedestrians around, but that day the whole area was for drifting only. It is a weekly routine. It is their second sport, of course, beside or rather after soccer.

The drifting starts with one young man speeding and then maneuvers and brakes and drifts with spectators cheering zealously, and then another driver and another. The whole of the afternoon and much of the evening go like this. Of course, during those events, some cars flip, drivers get injured, sometimes killed or even spectators get killed too. During my four years of stay in Saudi Arabia, I came to know of more than fourteen fatal accidents that involved an average of three fatalities per accident; one of them was a student at our college.

Does the government or the police step in to stop this madness? No. This is, as I mentioned before, perhaps the only freedom young people in Saudi Arabia have without any restraint. Is it a regulated sport? No. It is the young people's sport as my students proudly call it.

"Ustaz (Mr.) Sam, do you like to drift your car?" a friend of Ziad asked me one time. "Check me out on *YOUTUBE.COM*," he added

"No way. My car is not that good to withstand the pressure of drifting. I paid a lot of hard earned money for it," I replied humbly with a faint smile. "Besides, I think there is a lot of skill required to be able to drift, right guys? I don't have that skill as you do," I explained apologetically. When I visited "car drifting in Saudi Arabia" on *YOUTUBE.COM*, I was appalled.

***

I always wondered about how much it costs to repair and maintain cars that take part in those drifting events. However, some partial explanation was provided when one student named Muaaz sent me a message through one of his classmates excusing himself from attending the class that day telling me that he had to go and look for his car that was stolen three days earlier.

I asked one of his classmates "Look for it? Where? In the whole city?

He smiled and said "No, just near and around the three major drifting areas in Riyadh."

"What do you mean?" I asked.

Still smiling, he said "His car was stolen when he got out to buy something and someone jumped in and drove off on Sunday."

"Oh! You mean it was stolen to be used in drifting?" I asked.

"That's right."

"The police?" I asked naively.

"The police do not interfere in these matters. Doctor Sam, the police do not like to be in these matters of cars and we know the stolen cars go to drifting and then abandoned."

Two days later I saw Muaaz and I asked him about his car and he said he found it in one of the areas. It was roughed up but it was OK.

"I had to change all four tires as they were mangled and torn from the harsh drifting but everything else was fine, thank

God," he explained in a way that indicated that all of what happened was normal.

"Does this happen frequently that cars are stolen and used in drifting?" I asked tentatively. I was not sure of the question.

"Yes, all the time. Most cars are stolen for one purpose."

'For car drifting and drag race," I interrupted.

"Of course, the thieves are not real thieves. They just want to entertain us." He said with a smile and conviction of what he said as true.

***

It was just funny and strange to me. Muaaz was not mad that his car was stolen or abused at all. He felt his car did a role in making other young people have good time. And that was all that mattered to him. A strange feeling for us in America to accept or reconcile with.

As for a government crackdown on this seemingly harmless sport as Saudi young people see it (actually it is deadly to me), will stir anger among the youth and this is the last thing the government wants. If young people are happy, then why should the government risk a revolution or a popular uprising?

Chapter Thirty-Four

A Political Crackdown and Our Fears

The Arab spring was a curse to everybody everywhere. It brought a group of power seekers to leadership. It left chaos and devastation in Tunis, Egypt, Libya, Yemen, and Syria. So far Tunis and Yemen pulled out with minor damage to their economy and infrastructure. Civil unrest in Egypt continued even after the people there elected their first "democratically" elected president. Civil unrest and lawlessness in the streets of Egypt took a toll on the Egyptian economy and its relationship with a country like Saudi Arabia and the rest of the conservative Arab Gulf states, namely, the United Arab Emirates.

The Saudi government feared that Islamists of the Muslim Brotherhood of Egypt and their part-time allies, the Salafis of Egypt wanted to extend their revolution to neighboring Saudi Arabia. They wanted to set up the Islamic Caliphate once more. This is different from old Egyptian menace and danger to Saudi Arabia lingering since the fifties and sixties when Colonel Gamal Abdel Nasser actually wanted to change the regime in Saudi Arabia, but Nasser was a Socialist. Some members of the Muslim Brotherhood that overtook Egypt (and actually the elected president was a leading member of the Brotherhood) wanted to show their muscles in Saudi Arabia. The Saudi government reaction was quick and decisive. Many Egyptians and Syrians were arrested and severely tortured by Saudi authorities.

One of our colleagues in the English department was an Egyptian Islamist who disappeared suddenly and we never saw him again. We also heard that a Syrian professor working in the Education Department disappeared around the same time the Egyptian professor was gone. Their wives (and children, some of them were just babies and toddlers) came to the gates of the college for several days begging us to help them find their husbands. They would stand for a whole day asking every passerby if they knew their husbands. Their crying was heart-rending. They would even hold some of us to talk to but people were afraid to engage in any sort of conversation or show any sympathy. There were police informants nearby trying to find out who else was trying to help these women.

After a week we saw them no more. Rumors spread that the women were deported or jailed. Others whispered that after a woman's husband is dead or becoming absent for a certain period of time, she is legal to be married off to any man who claims her or simply she can be taken by any man. One colleague shrugged off some of the rumors while giving credence to others.

Chapter Thirty-Five

Some People Know the Truth about Islam

I met in early 2011 a Saudi colleague from another college but from the same university by the name of Omar Shabag. After a long discussion about linguistics and a new paper I submitted to a journal of linguistics in which he saw my name on the paper and recognized me. He asked me about "Optimality Theory and violable constraints" in the production of some vowels in English and how that affects Arabic learners of English. He remembered one key idea from my research paper namely, "The structural well-formedness of the output." He kept asking me questions that indicated he was really interested to learn something new. That week we met again and I brought to him more literature about the Optimality Theory that was bugging him. We also started talking about religions including Islam.

He confided to me that he comes from a family that rejected Islam for a very long time even though they had to put up an Islamic appearance. He told me that the prophet Muhammad was an opportunist who knew how to deceive the world and left behind him the most senseless followers. Those followers should learn, one way or another, using all media available, that Muhammad, their leader, was nothing more than a tribesman who coveted power and women and children. He is NOT sacred, nor a prophet, nor messenger from Allah; Allah himself is Muhammad's creation. He also said that his knowledge about the untruthfulness, falsehood, and fabrication of Islam is a long family tradition and a secret knowledge that they inherited from one generation to another since the time of Muhammad himself.

I wanted to engage in that discussion and learn more, but I was afraid. I did not know him enough. However, he told me that there were government spies around and he named few. He also told me of an incident that took place in his department few months earlier when an informant ratted on a colleague who ended up killed mysteriously. I was not sure what he was telling me all this for.

There was to my chagrin a person whose name was also Omar who would try to open conversations about silly topics, but he also was the kind of person who would accommodate to everybody's opinions and I knew he was a hypocrite who would show piety and religiosity and behaves as a good Muslim but in reality he was very corrupt. Whenever he approached me or talked to me, I just listened to him nodding my head up and down, right and left till the right moment comes to run away from him making no sound. I also thought he might be trying to entrap me. Knowing he was a phony, I always tried to avoid him. Tim also warned me about him. It just worried us. But the information from the first colleague about Muhammad and Islam was important to me.

Chapter Thirty-Six

William Carlos Williams - No Text Is Sacrosanct

Poetry is a great relief to me. When there is a discussion with students during class time or outside the classroom, they often quote the Quran as reference to back up a point they are trying to make. More often than not, the quote has nothing to do with the point in discussion. Sometimes, it is even counter to their point of view. However, they grew up in a culture where the Quran is not only sacred but also used to settle an argument. The one who has evidence from the Quran wins. They told me the Quran is eternal, final, and decisive. It is a text and a text cannot be changed, challenged, or emulated in any way possible. A written text is set in stone and remains untouchable forever.

So in my usual way of broadening the scope of their perception and making them think differently and perhaps destroy some taboos, I did something not many people have done. I demonstrated to them in practice how a text can be reshaped, even emulated, and crafted anew. My goal was to make them see that there is no holiness in a text for ever. I showed them that anything can change and can evolve due to circumstance, intentions and need.

I presented to them the beautiful poem "This Is Just to Say" by William Carlos Williams and after analysing the poem and savouring it, I presented to them a parody that I wrote. The original poem is easy to grasp, funny, but sort of sexist.

The poem is about a husband's wicked enjoyment of eating some plums that his wife has left in the refrigerator to cool.

This Is Just To Say   by William Carlos Williams

I have eaten
The plums
That were in
The icebox

And which
You were probably
Saving
For breakfast

Forgive me
They were delicious
So sweet
And so cold

After reading and explaining the poem, the students laughed, and they really savored the joke in the poem, but their biggest kicks came from the fact that the poet did that to his wife; perhaps pretty much like what some men would feel in the United States. However, that was not all. I tried to reverse the joke and gave them a parody of the poem. I wrote that myself in 2006 while working in a college in Virginia. Here is the other version of the poem supposedly a reply by the wife of William Carlos Williams as I imagined she would react to her husband's note on the refrigerator.

This Is Just Today   by Sami Benjamin

You have eaten

The plums

That were in the

Ice detox

And which

I was provably

Using

For an experiment

Don't blame me

They were pernicious

So septic

And so acid.

I showed practically to the students that any text can be imitated. "Any text," I stressed "No matter how sophisticated, religious, or sacred it is." That was new to them. No one has ever said that to them. They always thought that a text remains unchallenged forever. My goal of course was to prove to them that the Quran is just a text like any other.

To attenuate the impact of what I said lest they accuse me of blasphemy I used a lot of jokes and sense of humor in class to divert any potential anger. Thus, they only expressed their concerns that a woman should not say that to her husband. "A woman should not get even in this way," some students objected, raising doubts that I support women rights. I joked a lot about this and categorically denied that accusation quoting my support for men all the way to the end of eternity, no matter what that might cost. One student with a scowl face but in a facetious and humorous mood said "Women would hear about the poem and that would encourage them to retaliate whenever they have a chance." We all laughed. The resentment was so high that I had to ask, "Do you think a woman can make such a reply?" They all agreed that it was impossible and at this point everyone was happy and calm. However, later in the discussion, the students were less sharp about criticizing women when they realized that it was the husband's fault in the first place since he was the one who started it. They all then came to the conclusion that the wife's reply was legitimate. That was another day I saved myself from harm as I could not separate my Western mentality of supporting equal rights among all human beings and what I should do in that society that cannot tolerate others because of their religion or gender, among other things. I was angry myself that some young men never liked to see women win.

As I explained in the previous chapters, the Quran is a linguistic miracle. For Saudi students to see another text that would emulate the Quran in its wonder was a far-fetched thought. I deliberately explained the rhetorical prowess of some American and British literary works and even Arabic texts that Saudi students hardly had a chance to study or read. In a drama course, I comprehensively spent a lot of time commenting on the beauty of Shakespeare's linguistic dexterity. For example, in *Hamlet*, Act III, Scene IV, Hamlet says to his mother:

Look here, upon this picture, and on this,
The counterfeit presentment of two brothers.
See, what a grace was seated on this brow;
Hyperion's curls; the front of Jove himself;
An eye like Mars, to threaten and command;
A station like the herald Mercury
New-lighted on a heaven-kissing hill;
A combination and a form indeed,
Where every god did seem to set his seal,
To give the world assurance of a man:
This was your husband. Look you now, what follows:
Here is your husband; like a mildew'd ear,
Blasting his wholesome brother. Have you eyes?
Could you on this fair mountain leave to feed,
And batten on this moor? Ha! have you eyes?

The students were especially impressed by the adroit style of Shakespeare. The image of "heaven-kissing hill" was so imposing that the students were in disbelief that there could be another text as powerful as the Quran. Extraordinarily, students memorized that whole passage and others and kept repeating them to me to my ecstasy. Students realized for the first time that the Quran is not the ultimate intoxicating text. Moreover, students were really elated and almost euphoric to know ideas in lines by Shakespeare such as:

"There is nothing either good or bad,

But thinking makes it so." (Hamlet, Act 2, Scene 2, Lines 250 and 251)

They realized for the first time there is wisdom in texts other than the Quran.

Chapter Thirty-Seven

The Rime of the Ancient Cameleer and the Quran

The great English poet S. T. Coleridge wrote a master piece titled *The Rime of the Ancient Mariner*. It is basically the story of a ship crew who lose their way in the ocean till they reach Antarctica. When a beautiful bird, an Albatross, leads them out and into the right course, one of the sailors shoots the bird with his bow. The crew does not seem to mind his heinous act. Later, as a punishment for their crime against nature, they are drifted into the doldrums where there is no wind at all and the ship is completely becalmed. They could not move for a long period of time where they suffer all sorts of moral, psychological, and physical humiliation and torture for their crime against nature.

I was surprised to know of a similar long poem and myth of two thousand years old about a Bedouin who was lost in the desert with his caravan till a nomad camel came out from nowhere and also led them out to a known trail in the desert. The poem is part of the oral tradition of the people of south Najd, in south-central Saudi Arabia. When the caravan reaches a safe place, they kill the nomad camel and eat it. The caravan travelers were so ecstatic with the meat of the camel. After they ate to their fill, they started throwing the feet of the camel in the air and kicking them high. Then, they gave the head and other remains to wolves. Strangely, the wolves did not eat the head of the dead camel or any other discarded parts. There was a line in the poem where it says that "the eyes of the dead camel kept looking at the cameleer who killed it. When they left early in the morning the eyes were shining and rolling as if looking for the tall thin cameleer."

When the caravan travels for another day, a strong sand storm rips the crew of forty-two apart and no one could see or hear the other. They all perished for their crime except one, the narrator. Their bodies were scattered by the wind as if "they were like mangled food left by cattle," one line said. Amazingly, these were the exact words that came in the Quran six hundred years after the poem was known in the Chapter of the Quran of "Al-Feel" or "The Elephant."

To my surprise also, much of the language of the poem which is considered part of the rich oral tradition of Saudi poetry is very similar to that of the Quran's diction and style.

Chapter Thirty-Eight

Reading History from Literature:

Can Literature Decode Our Times?

Radical fundamentalist Muslims use the Quran as their guide in all aspects of their life. However, they never question its reliability or authenticity. They take the Quran at its face value. They use the Quran in their casual conversation, to buy, to sell, to start teaching, to go to the bathroom and in every other part of their daily activities. They even pepper their speech with quotes from the Quran so as to show their religiosity, to gain credibility, or to simply invoke blessings from Allah.

Every Muslim I met in Saudi Arabia or outside affirmed to me that the Quran tells about the future and that it can reveal the future if you read it with full faith. Of course, I take that with a smile and a nod especially that I also heard that from some Christians, Jews and few other people from other faiths. In the classroom, when I teach literature, I find more explanation of human life in literature than in any scripture. I got into discussions with Saudi students who affirmed that wars and disasters have been predicted in the Quran, so I adopted a historical approach that I often used in my literature classes. This technique was a big save to me in the classroom. It also got Saudi students think outside the Quran parameters and guidelines.

Normally, it is a major challenge for every writing or literature instructor to inspire his or her students to think critically, generate ideas, and write persuasively for or against a topic while avoiding the traditional hackneyed topics such as "abortion" and "the legalization of marijuana." These are subjects that students have been writing on and reading about since tenth grade. There is little or no scope for critical thinking left for new ideas. In Saudi Arabia, the challenge was bigger.

The method I used, on the other hand, had definitely offered a tremendous source for me to introduce new ideas and to lead a good discussion on a persuasive, compare and contrast, cause and effect, process analysis, or the argumentative essay. The method is to compare a current or a real life situation to the content of a novel, a play, a short story, or a poem.

To adopt this method, I faced two challenges: First, what literary works to use and what events to match them with. Secondly, what to look for in those literary works for the sake of the discussion and to train students to think critically, innovatively, and creatively. In other words, the instructor will have to find a text that reflects a current or a contemporary issue. The instructor's knowledge, education, experience, and level of sophistication are major factors in making successful choices. The text selection may take into account the students' interests, familiarity, and exposure to certain literary works as well as current real life events. Shakespeare's *Julius Caesar* and *Macbeth* are well-known texts. Other texts such as Auden's "The Unknown Citizen" or Sophocles' *Oedipus the King* can be introduced as readings, then analyzed, and discussed while drawing similarities to contemporary situations and political leaders.

Here is what I did in an introduction to literature class and in a drama class:

1- I chose a text (a play or a poem, for example) and asked students to read it at home and sometimes I asked students to read shorter passages in class. In the case of Shakespeare's *Julies Caesar*, which is a play about the assassination of the top political leader, Caesar, at the hands of his immediate subordinates, I asked students to search the theories regarding the assassination of president Kennedy, who was also assassinated presumably at the hands of his immediate subordinates; then we engaged in an oral discussion in class about the historical similarities and differences between Kennedy's assassination and Julius Caesar's assassination.

2- I did not try to influence the students' beliefs and opinions. For example, in case of teaching Sophocles' *Oedipus the King* (a play about a king who made crucial mistakes that affected his country negatively because of bad information and wrong judgment) and if the students believed Oedipus and George W. Bush were completely different, then, students would argue to that effect to show how different they and their circumstances were. If they believed the two leaders were identical and committed the same errors, then there was a great discussion. A great persuasive essay was then ready to come out. In all cases, I tried not to bias the students' opinion one way or another.

Also in the drama course, I used Miller's *Death of a Salesman*; a good topic was analyzing Biff's character. I selected some passages from the play that revealed this character. Students then wrote a descriptive or narrative essay about a person they met in their life that bore similarities or differences to Biff. Another famous literary character that I used in the introduction to literature course was Mathilde from Maupassant's "The Necklace." The students compared and contrasted both Mathilde and Biff as two losers in life because of either their vanity or superficial attitude to life or for being victims of their circumstances; they also compared a real person they knew to one of these literary characters.

In the same course, we examined Auden's poem, "The Unknown Citizen." I asked students in the initial discussion to find instances from the text where Auden prophesied what we see today such as law enforcement surveillance, Credit Reports, Consumerism and the role of Commercials in making us a consumerist society, the role of the media in shaping our public opinion, etc. The method was very successful in making students use literature to understand life instead of depending solely on the Quran.

Literature's role in the life of students appeared for the first time as a mirror to life; students saw a real practical role of literature; enjoyment was an extra benefit and treat.

I encouraged students to explore further folkloric traditional poems and songs and even the Bible. Since there were no bibles in Saudi Arabia, I asked them to find one on the internet. I asked them to read the story of Samson and Delilah from the Bible and then compare that to President Clinton and Monica Lewinsky. The idea of juxtaposing the two stories and examining them shed light and helped them understand more both stories, but for the first time in the lives of those students they read the Bible.

1- This method is good for all levels of writing and even literature courses. For one reason, the method offers a new way of dealing with writing topics that promote literacy and Critical Thinking practices.

2- This method offers a new way of looking at literary works as useful practical tools to understand life and decode historical events. The assumption that art and literature are not useful and that they belong only to museums, libraries, and poetry reading sessions is not valid any more. Art and literature come alive as down-to-earth tools to understand life as a whole and to interpret its mysteries in all of its peculiar manifestations.

3- The contribution of this method to literacy and the promotion of the practice of critical thinking is vast and enormous in addition to the promotion and appreciation of literature as a powerful prophetic projection and prediction of life.

4- This is a method that enabled students and me to discuss political and social issues in a controlled unobtrusive manner. Comparing or contrasting both Oedipus and Bush can be discussed objectively as long as the text of the play and real historical events are similar or different, and it is up to students to find those points of similarity and points of departure freely in an objective academic atmosphere. In other words, this method is an indirect way of being political without being obtrusive or offensive as long as proof from textual and historical evidence is available for the discussion.

A literary work, or even any artistic expression such as a sculpture or a painting, is a live metaphor of life or a segment of it. Sophocles' *Oedipus the King* is a mortal figure of speech standing for political leaders and nations along history. The proximity between Oedipus' initial victory over the Sphinx is similar to Hitler's earlier victories. Many other current presidents of our time are also very similar to Oedipus and Hitler. Those leaders later bring agony and strife to their peoples and ultimately to all humanity because of their arrogance and ignorance. The difference is that Oedipus was enlightened by the truth at the end, and more importantly, he redeemed himself. Other dictators have not paid for their mistakes or redeemed themselves.

Thus, responding to a work of art is definitely one of those spontaneous responses that are important to practicing Critical Thinking although most instructors and students are not trained or encouraged to do so because of what false art such as pop music and violent movies have done to them, i.e. ruining their artistic appreciation of true art. I always tried to encourage the trend and practice of Critical Thinking and appreciating all great literary works. Therefore, I encouraged students to choose literary works, written in English and Arabic, and informally consider what they can decipher in our life, either in our personal life or on a national level. The result was amazing. I got a lot of comparisons and analyses that mesmerized me. For example, they found strong similarities between the abusive Muslim clerics in Saudi Arabia and the shallow cleric portrayed in Naguib Mahfouz's *The Thief and the Dogs*. I knew then that my students learned something different from what the Quran got them stuck into.

I would like to close this chapter with the following poem by W. B. Yeats; he had predicted a nightmarish scenario of anarchy and darkness where a beast comes out of the desert to ruin human civilization:

The Second Coming

Turning and turning in the widening gyre
The falcon cannot hear the falconer;
Things fall apart; the centre cannot hold;
Mere anarchy is loosed upon the world,
The blood-dimmed tide is loosed, and everywhere
The ceremony of innocence is drowned;
The best lack all conviction, while the worst
Are full of passionate intensity.
....
The darkness drops again but now I know
That twenty centuries of stony sleep
Were vexed to nightmare by a rocking cradle,
And what rough beast, its hour come round at last,
Slouches towards Bethlehem to be born?

The prediction in the poem is eerie and uncanny and sends a scary chill down my spine. I feel Islamic radicalism is coming out to destroy all human civilization and replace it with Islamic Sharia law.

Chapter Thirty-Nine

Religion VS Literature

It was a fateful and decisive one class that clenched everything for me. It was the second (spring) semester of the year 2011-2012. It was the last semester I taught in Saudi Arabia. It was again an Introduction to Literature course. That semester, I decided to up the antes a bit. It is noteworthy to remind readers that literature is looked down upon in the Quran. Why? There is a verse in the Quran, among several, that directly lashes out at "poets" for being insidious, immoral, liars, depraved, and alluring. The verse is:

"And poets only deviants follow them; Do you not see them in every valley going astray? And that they say what they do not do?" (Al-Shoaraa, 224-226)

Undaunted by all this, I started the class as usual by asking few questions about the value of art and literature in humans' lives and even in animals and plants development. The students gave some positive answers. I then differentiated between art and non-art. I also stressed the value and importance of true art in our lives.

Literature is beautiful and aesthetic; it is beauty that is different from all other beautiful objects in life, different from other things that are temporary, short-lived, transient, and ephemeral. The beauty of art is permanent and eternal.

The beauty of a good-smelling food is short-lived. The dish might be looking delicious and giving out good smell but all that will change once one finishes the food. Think of a great cake or a delicious turkey before eating and right after finishing the dish. How about a new suit or dress? It would also age and wear out after some time. On the other hand, a painting, a classic song, a statue, a novel, or a poem lasts perpetually giving wisdom and beauty for eternity.

***

How about religious texts? First of all, a religious text is a form of writing and that is why religious people and clerics hate literature. Literatures' beauty and wisdom are everlasting and universal for all humanity. Religious texts are for few people in few places. Literature tells you of human life in the past, in the present, and in the future. Religious texts are made up and reflect only a narrow view; it is about horror that one will see if one does not follow the commands of the cult's leader or the religion's supreme cleric.

Artists and writers know more about life while religious cult leaders make random guesses that are never realized. They pray in vain and if one of their prayers or wishes comes true, it is a mere chance, a coincidence that it happened. They pray to soothe our aching souls and numb our feelings, sensations, and angst. Religious cult leaders and their cronies prey on the weak-spirited, the faint-hearted and the feeble-minded. Literary works address the intelligent and the bright-minded.

Religious people pray in vain while art and literature supply us with food for the soul and widen the scope of our knowledge and experience.

When I was called to the dean's office the following morning, he played the whole lecture on tape. I was being tape-recorded. My fears were all true. I simply said "I was talking about the infidels' religions and at no point I mentioned Islam or Muslims."

The dean and the others present in the large office did not expect that answer and there was sudden relaxation all over, to my own relief.

"You mean you did not intend Islam when you mentioned religion," the vice-dean interrupted the silence. He was a very educated scholar, so sensitive and an amazing fellow.

"Of course, it was a general lecture about the differences between art and non-art and definitely religion is non-art," I said firmly, convincingly, and approvingly.

The vice-dean quickly said "Then there is no problem."

The dean looked at me and did not say anything.

Chapter Forty

Faith

Tim was a great companion and a friend in that foreign territory. We spent a lot of time together arguing, thinking, and reasoning, and despite our philosophical differences, he being an ardent Christian while I was a humanist, a man who believes a great deal in humanity and the welfare of human beings, we complemented each other intellectually. No one alone could be totally right.

We saw in Saudi Arabia a lot of faith in religion. Faith in Islam was the only mover and decider of all aspects of life in that country. It was difficult for us to explain why all that belief in the tenets of Islam despite the fact there was absolutely no proof of any, and I mean any claim of the Quran or the stories of the prophet Mohammad. Tim being a very religious Christian failed to explain faith to me and why he would believe in something. I, on the other hand, would not believe in any "old stories," I often teased him jokingly to stir a discussion.

Tim always affirmed that faith is unexplainable and it is a gift and a blessing. I replied by saying that it is a sign of naivety, retardation, simple-mindedness, and lameness. I challenged him to explain why all believers of all religions think there is a god in heaven. Where is that heaven? I asked him, adding that modern science just drew a picture of outer space and we all know what is there. "No Super Being lives there, Tim."

I saw many people who believed in extraterrestrial creatures or aliens. However, people believe in them for a reason, and Tim and I tried to find a correlation between faith in religion and possible aliens. I suggested that if we assume that there are or were aliens who came to earth at one point of time and that these aliens were good to mankind as in healing the sick, saving humans from natural disasters, and punishing bad people that could be one reason why the faithful strongly believe in heavenly power, God and angels, for example. On the other hand, some of those aliens might have been evil and wicked and tried to harm people in one way or another, then came the belief that there are devils and evil spirits.

Tim seemed to agree. I would accept the idea of aliens as long as it would explain the idea of God, angels, and devils. God, angels, and devils are pivotal concepts or entities that all religions revolved around for thousands of years and became intrinsic in the fabric of humanity. It is very ironical. It is very difficult to eradicate these concepts from faithful people. It is my theory that God, angels, and devils were actual aliens, and then they were carved with power of steel in the minds of humans, in their collective unconscious.

***

When I sensed that Tim was halfway into believing what I said, I wanted to test his knowledge further, so I asked how to explain the existence of hell in humanity's collective unconscious.

He said "All stars are made of fire and the plausible explanation is that some humans were kidnapped, some were dropped into the burning star, the rest were returned to earth intentionally or unintentionally to tell their folks what happened."

I could not agree more. And "How do you explain that association of God and angels with light?" I asked.

"Easy," he replied. "When aliens came, they came in space ships that used fuel and perhaps other driving power we don't know yet that illuminated the sky and all surroundings. You only need to look at our modern time fighter jet or the launching of a space rocket in Cape Canaveral in Florida and you would see how much light and fire emanate and spread around."

We seemed to agree on the basic explanations. We felt good that day.

When I tried the following day to test Tim further, I asked him if he had ever entertained the idea that humans on earth had actually come from outer space. He said right away, "What do you mean?" I said "Assume that we came as invaders from outside. Our ancestors for some reason came here after they felt they were being threatened on their planet, or their planet was threatened by some geophysical catastrophe such as an asteroid, so they wanted to save their species by transporting an Adam and an Eve to another livable planet and you know, Tim, the story told in the Bible. Yes. I mean we are aliens." Tim's eyes were wide open and he stared at me for a while and murmured but did not utter a word. I could see the confusion on his being. I calmed him down and added "Just think about it."

After a while I said "Maybe it wasn't an attempt to save their species but it was an act of forced exile, a retribution for some heinous crime done by those people who were transported to earth as punishment with the promise to carry them back when they would come out clean in their act and pay for their deeds. However, the situation changed when that civilization collapsed and thus these aliens were cut off from their planet and remained on this planet. Don't you think?" Tim opened his mouth. He said nothing and he stared through the window at the serene blue sky of beautiful March. After two days he came to me and said "Western civilization is really great because we can discuss theories and exchange ideas about faith and the universe freely without fear of being accused of blasphemy or apostasy." I could not agree more. "This is true," I confirmed. "We had though our dark ages in the past and let's hope this part of the world gets out of it soon."

Chapter Forty-One

Why Are Freethinkers, Intellectuals, and Religious Freedoms Important?

Humanity undoubtedly has suffered a lot more from religion than from agnosticism. There are far more people who have been tortured, maimed, and killed in the name of God and Allah than in the name of the devil. Throughout the history of mankind there have been more conflict, struggle, misery, sadness, desolation, agony, distress, suffering, tragedy, calamity, misfortune, heartbreak, catastrophe, disaster, clash, controversy, dispute, discord, encounter, fight, and war because of religion than because of all other things.

It is important that some of us remain as freethinkers and intellectuals, and that some level of secularism and skepticism should be fostered and practiced for the sake of humanity. Why? Freethinkers and intellectuals are the safety valves of humanity. There are three reasons. The first is for the welfare of the individual. Secondly, it is for the sake of a group or a nation. Thirdly, it is for the sake of the whole of mankind. This might sound strange or vague for some.

There are numerous incidents of individuals who suffered from terrible nervous breakdowns or deep depression because of their religiosity and sense of guilt for not doing enough to please their deity. There are many times when an individual feels that religion is a heavy burden: The rituals and ceremonies, the duties, the commitment, and the responsibility for a higher authority that never reports back to that individual while the poor individual waits and waits for a sign that he or she has done right or wrong but the feedback never comes through. What is worse is when a meaningless random occurrence is on the horizon and adds to the mess and confusion of the helpless individual who is just and abjectly in need of some communication from "above."

I helped in February 2006 a miserable woman who gave birth to a child out of wedlock, and because of her religious beliefs, she grew very despondent to a degree that she was famishing herself and her baby to death. She felt a great sense of guilt for what she considered a crime against her God and faith. I directly explained to her that there is absolutely no such brutal, heartless God. I showed her that religion is an emotional and a spiritual need inside us that we need to experience and seek and fill out our hearts with; we humans need to laugh or watch a football game; we also need religion. I told her we still need the values and ethics of a good human being and religion undoubtedly gives us a lot of those beautiful values and ethics.

We need to develop a conscience that can differentiate between what is right and what is wrong. I told her that she might have violated some social conventions that her society upholds tightly. Each society preserves some rules and norms that regulate the lives of its members, to protect them from chaos and anarchy. It is all relative and varies from one society to another. Social leaders or clerics then attach, sometimes, a heavenly touch or authority to those values and conventions and name it "God" to ensure that we will respect those values. I tried in my talk to her to downplay religion to a degree that indicated that religion is not real. At the end of my speech, that lady felt relieved from her devastating sense of guilt. I emphasized to her the importance of adhering to the good values of society and respecting all its norms to preserve law and order and to protect the members of society. Few weeks later I ran into that lady in the street. She was upbeat and happy; she looked very healthy and full of hope again. Her baby was even healthier.

***

A nation can fall into the hands of religious fanatics and radicals very easily. We have numerous examples over the history of mankind, and we know how the world suffered at the hands of religious extremists. Today the world witnesses terrorism beyond reason and all in the name of religion. It is very important that some of us should maintain some level of freethinking, secularism, and non-belief. Those individuals will serve as safety valves against extremism, namely religious extremism.

There are many countries in recent times where radicals are ready to invade another country in the name of Islam and Allah and they are not hiding their intentions. Imagine the disaster if they carry out their plans which they are openly preparing to do anyway. They need some wise voices amongst them to curb their madness. Millions in Egypt, Pakistan, Syria, Libya, Tunis, Algeria, Iran, India, Indonesia, Nigeria, Afghanistan, Morocco, Chechnya, and many more are ready to "crawl" or "march on" in the name of Allah and kill their enemies and the enemies of their religion, foreign or domestic and kill everyone who is not with them in order to die in the name of Allah.

***

As shown above, a whole nation can be readily suicidal in the name of a religion, namely Islam. To be specific, it is not the religion *alone* that drives everyone to the edge of insanity but there is evidence that radical clerics and preachers have a big role in that insanity. They are manipulating the masses to the verge of the destruction of humanity.

And that is my third concern: The future of mankind and human civilization. Religion can harm mankind, and the radicalized brand of Islam in particular is my concern since all the evidence points at that form of radicalized Islam as the engine that is pushing humanity to its madness and demise. In the case of that lady who felt so guilty for having committed a big mistake in her eyes because she violated her religious beliefs, we can imagine what would happen if everyone is pushed to self-destruction for breaking what seems a violation against God (who may not exist in the first place or at least not in the form and function handed down in some religions).

We then can imagine a whole nation turning to self-destruction and the destruction of another nation or nations to gratify their God or Allah and their radical religious beliefs. Thus Humanity as a whole, like an individual or a nation, is also at risk. Imagine if we all become so entrenched in our religious beliefs. Radical Muslims are intent on converting the whole world into their extreme brand of Islam to the embarrassment and objection of the sweeping majority of Muslims who are peaceful and moderate. Extremists believe their radicalized brand of Islam is the only religion that should dominate the world. This is one reason to foster some secularism and a great amount of religious freedom, especially in Muslim countries. Each individual, nation, and the whole of mankind must maintain a certain amount of secularism that functions as brakes or safety valves in case we all go religiously berserk.

Chapter Forty-Two

Sharia, Politics and Women Drive Ban

An old, burning issue in Saudi Arabia is whether women would be allowed to drive. It is noteworthy to mention that Saudi Arabia is the only country in the world that enforces a ban on women driving. There have been many demands on the part of women and human rights organizations to give women in Saudi Arabia the opportunity to exercise such a mundane practice that all women in the whole world have for granted.

There are Islamic scholars who have tried from a legislative and theological point of view to legalize driving on the basis of a common Islamic premise of precedents during the time of the Muslim prophet Muhammad which is whether women rode camels and horses on their own; the answer is "yes;" women during Muhammad's time rode camels and horses and even worked and fought side by side men; therefore, women, by the same token, can drive cars in modern day times. This Sharia Ijtihad (syllogism or deduction) did not sit well with the ultraconservative self-styled scholars of the Shura Council that oversees the implementation of Islamic rules and Sharia laws in the Kingdom.

Women groups inside Saudi Arabia and outside cite a lot of issues regarding the ban such as women suffering to find a humane and affordable means of transportation. Many women came out and said they wait for hours to find a taxi in the city. In the suburbs and in smaller cities, it is even worse. The dangers of being alone walking for miles is another reason that women groups cite as part of their suffering. Going to work, if allowed by their husbands or fathers, has become a nightmare for most working women. Taking children to schools is another horrific experience most women endure when it comes to finding a ready and comfortable means of transportation.

So what was the radical clerics' explanation? The ultraconservative officials of the Sharia Council claim that women driving will encourage premarital and extramarital sex. Preposterous! Their understanding is that when women can drive around, that will consequently enable them to go to places beyond their reach where they meet men and have sex. That was the clerics' explanation. Very naive as if one cannot have sex where she lives or just go to her neighbor's house which regularly happens a lot nowadays. It would be naive if one thinks there is no premarital sex in Saud Arabia. I secretly surveyed about 160 Saudi males and almost 59 % of them confirmed having sex with women they were not married to, mostly Saudi women and fewer foreign women.

***

However, the controversy of whether a woman's driving promotes premarital or extramarital sex or not is not the major issue. The serious issue involved is not an Islamic legislative or theological matter but rather a political matter that has to do with the balance of power in Saudi society and the Kingdom as a whole which is part of the government overall plan to keep everybody down and under control and in need all the time, men as well as women.

In other words, the Saudi government deemed it more convenient that siding with the ultraconservative clerics will have several benefits simultaneously: First, it will show the government as conservative and hence clerics will approve of the government; both the government and the ruling family need to assert this crucial position all the time. Secondly, the government ban will prove that the government is working hard to preserve the values of chastity and purity, very important principles in Islam. Third, that will keep everybody busy, preoccupied, and exhausted (literally and not metaphorically); in that way, some attention is diverted away from the ruling family and the government members who are often criticized for being liberal or not paying enough attention to Islamic values. In other words, that is how the rulers of Saudi Arabia find it safer to be radical and show keenness in preserving the values of the true fundamentalist Muslim society. However, it is believed that at one point women in Saudi Arabia will gain their right to drive if they persist and get moral support from international human rights organizations.

Chapter Forty-Three

The State of Saudi Women in Particular and Muslim Women in General

We in the West see Muslim women through our Western eyes. We do not see them in their cultural environment or from their historical perspective. It is surprising then to know, after a long investigation on my part and from other scholarly proven surveys and studies, that the majority of Muslim women are comfortable the way they are treated in their societies. They accept their fate as Allah's commandment and feel complacent about their low position in society because they will be generously rewarded for that in paradise. Their complacency and compliance were a big surprise to me, almost a shock.

The most obvious aspect of Muslim women is when we see them with the traditional head cover or the veil. Where does that come from? Before I answer, I must admit that there are many other sects and religions that instruct women to cover their hair or heads, namely, Orthodox Jewish women and some Orthodox Christian Churches such as Greek, Roman, Russian, to name a few, where women cover their hair or heads. It turns out that there is no direct commandment in the Quran. The closest verse is:

"And tell believing women.......to lower their scarves to their chests and not to show their adornment." (Al-Nour, 31)

In this often quoted verse by radicals as the order for women to cover hair and face, there is no actual directive to that effect by the wildest imagination. In the same Chapter of the Quran, Al-Nour, there are several direct references to "vaginas' and to other "private parts" and it would have been possible to mention "hair" or "face" if they needed to be covered as well. The words "vaginas" and "bottoms" are generously made mention of in the Quran and in that specific Chapter, Al-Nour.

However, there is still something peculiar to Muslim women's appearance and status. And that is whether Saudi women and Muslim women in general have a choice. The answer is no. Unlike women of other religions and societies (e.g., Jews and Eastern Orthodox Christians), Muslim women have to abide by both clerics' orders and society's norms. A double vice, so to speak. They have no choice whatsoever. And that what riles us in the free world. We feel that Muslim women have no choice.

The broad question is "What do Muslim women living under Islamic Sharia law in general and Saudi women in particular have?" Another question is "What don't they have?" In other words, what are their rights? According to the Quran, they get a dowry when they get married. They are entitled to inheritance at a half share of a male brother, for example. They can file for divorce. They can own their own property and manage their own money.

On the other hand, a man can marry more than one woman and up to four at any given time. He can divorce instantly unlike a woman who has to file and that can take years till a judge decrees a divorce if the judge sees a good reason. Worst of all, social traditions in many cases suspend Sharia law for a woman, and thus, she may lose access to her inheritance or even her money. It is a man's right to prevent a woman from leaving the house her entire life. That man can be a father, a brother, a husband, a son, an uncle, or any man who becomes custodian of a woman in the absence of her immediate male family members. So it is a catch 22 for women. They have the right to own but they may not have control or access to manage what they own. Only few women in Saudi society are in charge of their property. Most women have deputized (by issuing a proxy or right of attorney kind of document) their husbands, sons, or brothers to handle their transactions from as simple a task as opening a bank account to managing a multi-national company. Of course many women lose much of their wealth as a result.

***

Moreover, women under Sharia law cannot get a job unless their male custodian grants them that right which can be withdrawn at any time he sees appropriate. Women cannot travel or get education without their custodian's consent. I am not talking about under age women who want to travel or go to school. No. A woman who is fifty years old will still need a custodian's consent to do any of the above, i.e., to travel, to get a passport, to enter school or college or even to buy a cell phone. Women cannot drive cars in Saudi Arabia and Afghanistan during Taliban rule and even after ten years of deposing the Taliban regime.

Hajj (the annual pilgrimage to Mecca) is the holiest part of Islam's worship. Ironically, Saudi women are not allowed, or to put it more accurately, not encouraged to perform this highly appraised part of Islam for a quirky paradox. The paradox is two-fold: The first is that those who perform Hajj will get eternal forgiveness or absolution of guilt and sin as Hajj automatically grants permanent remission of wrongdoing as the Quran says; secondly, to perform Hajj, women have to uncover their faces as a conditional part of the Hajj itself but traditions and social rules (and radical interpretation of the Quran) do not allow women to remove the face cover. A very odd situation for women. Saudi men do not like to see their women bare their faces or get forgiveness, but rather, they like to keep them in guilt and behind the veil.

My final conclusion is that Muslim women, ironically like Muslim men, are completely under the spell of their religious instructions or, specifically, oppression. It is a set of instructions derived from the Sharia Law and the social conditions that ruled the setting for thousands of years. They are bound by them seemingly forever. The Quran orders women to obey men while giving men the upper hand at the same time. This is the situation of women under Sharia law. It is not strange that women are only seen walking in from-head-to-toe black garment in the streets of Saudi Arabia. They are not allowed even to talk to any male stranger. The women in Afghanistan, Somalia, and many other communities in Muslim countries live in similar conditions.

Furthermore, women add more pressure on women and make life harder for them. How? For example, a mother-in-law will push her son to bar his wife from getting a job or access her money. The mother-in-law would taunt her son to be a man and stand up like a man against his wife if the latter wants to own a property. Hardening a husband's heart against his wife is common practice in the Muslim society (We have similar situations like these in our Western societies though). Mothers would be in many cases so harsh on their daughters just out of fear for them or fear from a husband or a father. In other words, mothers justify their practice by saying that they are doing this for fear of consequences from the patriarch in the family.

Chapter Forty-Four

Can Muslim Women Play Sports?

How free are Muslim women in their daily life? I am not talking about dating, choosing a husband, or getting a job. I am talking about exercising, swimming, shopping, visiting friends (female friends only), reading the news, buying a dress or a pair of shoes, watching TV or owning a laptop with internet connection. These activities that we take for granted in the West are difficult to come by for women in conservative Muslim societies. How about taking part in sports competitions? In Saudi Arabia, Afghanistan, and Somalia, women cannot compete in sports. However, a change happened recently.

The biggest change happened in the London Summer Olympic Games of 2012. For the first time in the history of Saudi Arabia, the Saudi government allowed two Saudi women to compete. However, the first ever two Saudi women athletes to represent Saudi Arabia in the Olympic Games have been treated really badly by the people of their country; they were snubbed by their nation's media and subjected to a campaign of ridicule and hate by their fellow citizens, men and women.

Sarah Attar ran the 800 meters on the Olympic Stadium track and Wojdan Shaherkani competed in judo earlier in the Games. It is notable to mention that the Saudi government eased its strict stance on women competing following international pressure. The representation was symbolic for

Saudi women, but it was a milestone. However, this came at a heavy price. When the two women athletes went back to the Kingdom of Saudi Arabia, they did not receive a heroines' welcome. Instead, they found complete avoidance from even friends and relatives. Why? Because according to Islamic extremist Wahabi rules, they desecrated the honor of Muslim women.

Apart from the not-so-impressive achievement of the two athletes, due in part to the fact that they never had a chance to compete or train or even get decent training equipment, medical or nutritional care, no Saudi newspaper had mentioned them in any news item, and no Saudi TV channel had either.

Social media such as Twitter and Facebook were different in Saudi Arabia. The two female athletes were noticed and received a lot of attention. They were called the "prostitutes of the Olympics" and the "Shame of the Kingdom." All sorts of filthy language were used in connection with the two hapless women athletes. The attack came from both men and women. So instead of seeing their participation as a step forward in the direction of equality and freedom for women and female athletes, women in Saudi Arabia saw a setback in their struggle. Things did not change at all for women in a positive way.

***

I learned further that sports for women and girls in schools and colleges are frowned upon.

"Is there a reason for that?" I asked a Saudi man in the Yamama Mall in Riyadh.

"It's obscene, immoral and disrespectful to religion," he said in a firm tone.

"Yes, I see," I concurred in my sarcastic manner and added "But how immoral and disrespectful, brother?"

"They jump, and run and roll on the floor like snakes. Very disgusting. They wear little clinging clothes. Not Islamic in any way," he confirmed.

"That's true. I see what you mean," I agreed with much restrained resentment and anger inside me. I had no choice lest I should risk injury from a punch or arrest by the religious police if I disputed what he said.

In Saudi Arabia, there is always a hanging fear of a religious or social backlash. Any small act can bring about one or both of such backlash or negative reaction.

Chapter Forty-Five

Democracy in Saudi Arabia

There is no Western style democracy in Saudi Arabia. There is though a much diluted form of parliamentary system of one chamber in the Kingdom. It is called the Shura Council or Consultative Council. It can discuss laws and legislation but it does not draft or pass binding laws or legislation. Its role is mere decor for the world. It is a rubber stamp body of representatives who have never opposed the ruling family's interests or the Saudi government's demands.

King Abdullah is in my opinion and in the opinion of so many is a reformist but he is very cautious, as I pointed out before, not to anger the conservative clerics and extremist preachers who are waiting for a royal mistake to turn against the ruling family.

The king in February of 2012 announced that the women will make up for no less than 20 percent of the 150 members of the Council. This is a revolutionary leap for women in Saudi Arabia. That means that women were granted suffrage; they will be allowed to run for elections and vote for the first time in Saudi history. The news was greatly welcomed by fewer women than expected. A large portion of Saudi women, ironically, saw this as a "deviation from Allah's Sharia and not so Islamic." said one woman on Twitter.

Men were not so impressed either. Extremists and fundamentalists (basically identical) were very nervous.

They saw this as a threat to the structure of the "true Islamic traditions and it will undermine the rule of Allah in the land of the prophet Muhammad."

Moreover, King Abdullah seems to be facing resistance inside his own family sometimes. Some royal family members see liberalization as a threat and a step towards weakening their grip over the reins of the kingdom. It seems that "the Council has been a rubberstamp and will continue to be a rubberstamp," affirmed one Saudi blogger in March of 2012. The King is leading a balanced and calculated modernization and liberalization and fewer family members support that move.

This is being carried out to let the Saudi people vent some steam and simultaneously allay Western criticism of the Kingdom's record of human rights violations and lack of freedom. In that respect, the King affirmed in his speech that "the reforms are in line with our Islamic values." He had to make this statement to reassure all interested and involved constituents and parties, namely, members of the ruling family, the extremist clergy, the West, liberals, conservatives, Saudi women, and Saudi men. A very tight rope that he is walking. Time will show who will buy this and who will not!

Chapter Forty-Six

Who Rules Saudi Arabia?

The women driving ban is a test of power that shows who is the boss. It is not a test of power between men and women. On the contrary, the majority of men are indifferent to that issue. They do not object much to seeing their wives and daughters driving cars. The test of power is between the ruling monarch and his family on one hand and the ultraconservative groups on the other. Those radical groups have a strong pull in Saudi politics. Therefore, each side tries to be more pious than the other. Each side tries to appear as more conservative than the other. There is a fine line the ruling family has to walk. King Abdullah is a reformist somehow, but he does not want to anger the already scowling rigid ultraconservative clerics or some dissenting members of his family.

The monarchy in Saudi Arabia understands the importance of a marriage of convenience between religion and politics and they are good at that. The ruling family knows very well how to wield political Islam into the lives of the masses in Saudi Arabia. Political Islam simply means incorporating the teachings of Islam into the daily lives of the people, but always, this is done to the benefit of the ruling family. For example, the banking system is all Islamic in the sense that people deposit their money in banks but there is no yield or interest paid out. Why? Because that would be usury, a forbidden practice in Islam. No one can lend money and gets return for that. Moreover, when one deposits his or her money by way of investment, he or she may lose the principal altogether. Why? Because Islam allows that since one is likely to gain or lose. This is called the Islamic system of banking. I know of many helpless individuals who lost all of their money because of that. Banks are owned by the ruling sheiks and run by their cronies who make billions out of the misery of the masses.

Similarly, the ruling family knows how to use Political Islam to hold to power. How? First, there is no constitution in Saudi Arabia. Second, there are no democratic elections. Third, there is no transition of power. Fourth, there is no transparency on financial revenue of the state. Fifth, there are no checks and balances of any measure. Why? Because Islam gave full authority to the Muslim Leader to decide what is good for Islam, and the rulers know well how to appear as the pious Muslims and hence continue to stay in power. This is very similar to the European monarchies in the Middle Ages when the king was God's shadow on earth.

Chapter Forty-Seven

The Legitimacy of Illegitimacy

How do Arab and Muslim regimes justify their rule without any democratic elections or laws? In other words, how do the rulers of Saudi Arabia, Jordan, Morocco, Oman, etc. gain their legitimacy? The answer is deep down in the *Imara* (ruling) system or Caliphate (succession) system. It is a system that is based on passing down the reins of the state from one Muslim ruler to another in the name of Islam and Allah. So where does that come from? It comes from the *Ashari* doctrine. One may call it the Islamic constitution that regulates accession to power in purely Islamic fashion.

In the *Ashari* doctrine, history stops for Allah alone and, therefore, it is absolute and because Islam is Allah's revelation, then the Muslim ruler is absolute in his rule since he represents Allah. That is more than constitutional legitimacy; it is Allah's legitimacy or mandate bestowed upon the Muslim ruler. Hence, Muslim rulers support the conservative approach of the Asharites and in turn the Ashari thought serves the rulers a good turn in consecrating their absolute rule. That also explains why Muslim countries reject modernism; it is because the idea of absolutism that was given by Allah to the Islamic state; there is no need for anything that is not Islamic. That explains also why Muslim countries are against modernism and prefer to remain underdeveloped.

The Ashari doctrine was founded by Abu Al-Hasan Al-Ashari (d. 945 CE). The influence of the Asharites on

Islamic theology is by far the most important. All the Islamic fundamentalist radical theologians such as Al-Ghazali (d.1111), Ibn Taymiyyah (d. 1328) and others are the product of that school of thought. The Asharites limited their world and religious knowledge to the strict interpretation of the Quran and the traditions of the Prophet Muhammad. A Muslim, therefore, should follow a very strict tradition of obeying the commands of trusted Muslim scholars alone (Ulema) who are in turn appointed by the Muslim absolute ruler. For the Asharites, humans have no power to change the world and there is no knowledge beyond what is mentioned in the Quran. They claim (every radical Muslim would say the same today) that the Quran has got absolute knowledge of everything one might need to know in the world.

***

Moreover, in the Ashari doctrine, the individual, the human being, is nothing more than a tool in the realm of the Muslim ruler; therefore, the individual is a servant to the ruler who, in turn, serves Allah and the Quran. There is neither individual freedom, field for contemplation, nor a chance for creativity in the Ashari thought. There is only the fixed frame of the Quran, the only reference for the individual.

The individual for the Asharites has no absolute free will, only freedom of intention. Only Allah has the will and the power, and humans have to obey Allah's will. Therefore, the individual is not supposed to question the behavior of the ruler or his commands as the ruler is chosen by Allah. In other words, the ruler could hide behind the name of Allah and rules absolute. Muslim rulers have used the Ashari doctrine in this manner.

The Asharites and their followers count in their call for Muslims to abide by their monarchs and comply with their rule on a verse in the Quran that forthrightly orders Muslims to do so. The verse says:

> "O those who have believed, obey Allah, and obey the Messenger (Muhammad), and obey those in authority among you (in charge of you). And if you disagree over anything, refer it to Allah and the Messenger, if you should believe in Allah and the Last Day. This is the best option and for the best outcome."
>
> (Al-Nisaa, 59)

The West, on the other hand, believed in humanism, rationalism and the evolution of history. That explains why the West developed. There are two worlds: One Islamic world that is frozen in history and one Western that is evolving; one Islamic world that petrified and one Western world that cogitates; one Islamic world that is dead and one Western world that is alive. The West is energetic and is not limited by absolute doctrines from the past. The Islamic world cast itself into a granite belief and did not move on in history. It refused to look beyond its borders of thought; it consumed itself in the absolute beliefs of the Quran.

***

So now how do Muslim rulers justify their illegitimate rule? They wear the mask of Allah. Their political injustice and despotism are part of the Asharites', Al-Ghazali's, and Ibn Taymiyyah's radical call to obey the Quran and its Muslim protector, the Muslim ruler. That explains why Muslim radicals do not respect human rights, democracy, the arts, modernity, creativity, etc.

Chapter Forty-Eight

Wahabism and Political Islam

The term Political Islam can be summed up in the attempt of Muslim fundamentalist groups to establish an Islamic society where the rules of the Quran and the Teachings of the Prophet (Sunnah) are strictly applied. This implies the application of the traditional way of life in all aspects of life, economic, social, legal, jurisprudential, political, and every other aspect in the life of Muslims.

The roots of *modern* political Islam can be traced back to the Asharites of the tenth century and Ibn Taymiyyah (born 1263, Ḥarran, Mesopotamia—died Sept. 26, 1328). The Ashari Doctrine and Al-Ghazali shaped Ibn Taymiyyah himself. However, *traditional* Political Islam started right with Mohammad in the sixth century. From the first day of Islam, Muhammad was political, his wars, his alliances, his establishment of a state; the Quran itself is considered a constitution for many Islamic groups. The Asharites and Al-Ghazali were the link between the prophet Muhammad (the old school of political Islam) and Ibn Taymiyyah (the new school of political Islam). Both schools are identical in doctrine, just used different means to adapt to different circumstances and times.

Ibn Taymiyyah is one of the most rigid theologians of Islam. His impact on present day terrorists is far more forceful than anyone else in the history of Islam. His teachings and views hardened many present day Muslims to the degree that millions of Muslims want to live the early traditions of Islam with their rigidity and intolerance. More ominous, they want to spread this way of life to every part of the world. Ibn Taymiyyah wanted Islam to return to its origins (the Quran and Sunnah) and nothing else. Modernism even by the standards of his time (13th/14th Centuries) is evil and against the will of Allah and the teachings of Islam.

Ibn Taymiyyah had firm struggle against Shiah Islam, Suphism (mysticism), philosophy, Christianity, Judaism, and Kalam (Dogmatic Theology or logic). He considered Shiites a threat to Islamic traditions. He strongly attacked the practice of visiting the graves of the dead and denounced the worship of saints (aowliyaa) as being against religious law (Sharia). He attacked philosophers and logicians because they think rather than copy from the Quran and the Prophet's Sayings and Traditions. Suphis believed in the union of God and man in one. Thus, this *Ityhadiyyah* or monism or oneness of the Suphis was to Ibn Taymiyyah an evil that should be prevented by all means. Therefore, he considered Suphism an aberration of Islam that should be fought against.

Strangely, he came up with anthropomorphism which means ascribing human characteristics to God. This idea did not sit well with many theologians of his time. Therefore, he was punished and imprisoned for that for long periods of time. In all, Ibn Taymiyyah style of writing and speaking was marked by brilliant polemic and extensive documentation from the Quran and Sunnah (the Prophet's sayings) and that established the core of his doctrine on Islamic Government system: everything must be in strict accordance to The Quran and Sunnah.

***

His most important views are that *Igmaa* or social consensus was of no value to run a state or solve issues of the Muslim community. Therefore, democracy for him and later for the rulers of Saudi Arabia and Muslim leaders in other parts of world are not for the good of the world. Moreover, Ibn Taymiyyah, being a true fundamentalist, wanted everything in a Muslim community to be run and done in accordance to traditional, fundamentalist Islamic practice "as if the Prophet Muhammad will do it himself." Thus, Ibn Taymiyyah wanted every Muslim ruler to apply strictly Sharia law and rely on it for running the state.

What makes it hard for present day rulers in Saudi Arabia is not only applying Sharia law but it is what Ibn Taymiyyah added. He says "if the ruler does not apply the religious law literally and thus disobey Allah, the Muslims must rise against the ruler and depose him right away." That explains the rigidity of the rulers of Muslim countries and why they compete to be very radical.

No other Muslim theologian has influenced present day Muslims more than Ibn Taymiyyah. No fundamentalist movement or terrorist movement has not been influenced by the teachings of Ibn Taymiyyah and inspired by his thought. Bin Laden and Al-Qaeda, the Islamic Jihad, the Muslim Brotherhood of Hassan Al-Banna, the Salafy (fundamentalist) Movement, Algamaa Al-Islamiya (the Islamic Group) and all present day Muslim militant groups (Islamic State of Iraq and Levent or ISIL is being formed) are basically trying to establish a traditional society strictly similar to that of the early Islamic society using all means to establish that goal and having the Perfect Islamic State as envisaged by Ibn Taymiyyah.

Twentieth century influential Islamic radical similar to fourteenth century Ibn Taymiyyah is Sayed Qutb (1906-1966). He draws the line between what is Islamic and what is debauchery and apostasy. Applying Islamic Sharia law exclusively derived from the literal interpretation of the Quran and Sunnah is the only guarantee of "a true Islamic society." Any secularism, liberalism, or copying from the West, which Qutb detested, will turn a Muslim society to "a barbaric pre-Islamic Jahili (ignorant) society."

The same thoughts had been echoed by other radical Islamic theologians such as Maulana Sayyid Abul Ala Maududi (1903-1979), founder of Pakistan's radical Jamaat-i-Islami. Like Qutb, he promoted Jihad against non-Muslims. "The whole world should be ruled by Islamic Sharia law, and Muslims should not copy any Western ways of life," he said.

It is a fact that every Muslim fundamentalist believes that, according to Abul Ala Maududi, "Allah ordained a commandment to all Muslims to fight and kill non-Muslims so as to replace man-made law in the West and in the East by God's Law, the Sharia, and Islam has conquered the entire world." It is important to note that Muslim extremists and radicals will put on smiles and behave courteously until the time comes for the Islamic revolution that the Muslim leader Abul Ala Maududi predicted.

Here is Abul Ala Maududi in his own words saying:

> "In reality Islam is a revolutionary ideology and programme which seeks to alter the social order of the whole world and rebuild it in conformity with its own tenets and ideals."

There is a remarkable historical similarity between fourteenth century Ibn Taymiyyah and twentieth century Qutb and Maududi: Ibn Taymiyyah saw the invasion of the Islamic world by the Crusaders and then by the Mongols; Baghdad fell to the Mongols in 1258 and later Damascus. Ibn Taymiyyah always claimed that Muslims were weak because of their staying away from true fundamentalist application of the Quran and Sunnah teachings in their lives. Likewise, Sayed Qutb saw in his early years the fall of the last Islamic Caliphate in Istanbul and the official end of the Islamic Empire during and right after the end of World War I. Abul Ala Maududi saw Muslims in India under British rule and later suffering at the hands of the Hindus. Both Qutb and Abul Ala Maududi saw Western modernization and economical superiority as danger to Islam, and, like Ibn Taymiyyah, they claimed that Muslims' staying away from true fundamentalist application of the Quran and Sunnah as the lead cause of Muslims' weakness. Qutb and Abul Ala Maududi justified "jihad against non-Muslim societies for their secularism and debauchery."

Eighteen century Muhammad Ibn Abdel Wahab in Arabia saw the same conditions. By the standards of the eighteenth century, he believed Western enlightenment, industrialism and freedom posed a great danger to the Islamic world. British and French imperial movement was a scare to Abdel Wahab. Moreover, the Ottoman Turks, whom Ibn Abdel Wahab detested, invaded all Arabia and other Muslim countries which was devastating for him. Therefore, it was not strange that he echoed the same message of Ibn Taymiyyah: Strict application of Sharia law literally derived from the Quran and Sunnah to protect Muslims and be able to take over the lands of the infidels. Strangely, all these theologians could not understand that Sharia is not the solution to their social problems but rather modernization, economic and technological development as the way out like Japan and Germany did after WWII, for example.

Instead, radical Muslims believe that they can take the world by violence and by Wahabi ideology. Qutb expressed that idea of "a shortcut to take the world since Allah is on Wahabis side. Scientific and economical excellence would take a lot longer and the West is already ahead," Qutb Affirms. Therefore, the radical ideology is the best option.

As I mentioned before, Wahabi Islam was the inspiration to Qutb and Abul Ala Maududi, and is by far the primary religious movement behind present day extremist Islam.

It would be a philosophical mistake and an unethical argument to criticize all of Islam on the basis of doctrines peculiar to Ibn Taymiyyah, Wahabi Muslims or twentieth century teachings of Qutb and Abul Ala Maududi. There are tolerant Muslims and there is peaceful Islam, but the serious matter is that there is an increasing number of Muslims who adhere to the teachings and methods of Ibn Taymiyyah, Abdel Wahab, Qutb, and Abul Ala Maududi. And that is the danger to human history and modern civilization.

Chapter Forty-Nine

Wahabism: Silent Terrorism, Islamic Determinism, and Terror on Demand

It is clear that I have left Wahabism to the end of my presentation of political Islam intentionally. There are four reasons for that decision:

- First, eighteenth century Wahabism was the historical and doctrinal bridge between Ibn Taymiyyah of the fourteenth century and both Qutb and Abul Ala Maududi of the twentieth century.

- Secondly, Wahabism is the first successful application of political Islam ideas and doctrines of Ibn Taymiyyah and Abdel Wahab in a Muslim society, Saudi Arabia.

- Thirdly, it is the living epitome of what is called extreme Islam; in other words, it is the enduring model of political Islam that survived all odds. It is noteworthy to mention that Saudi Arabia is the perfect example where the state is Wahabi. Afghanistan under Taliban was another model.

- Fourth, it is the inspiration to all modern-day movements by Muslim extremists around the world as it sums up, so to speak, an ideal traditional Islamic society that every extreme fundamentalist Muslim dreams of. Wahabism is alive in Egypt, Syria, Palestine (Hamas), Libya, Tunis, Algeria, Morocco, Yemen, Pakistan, Afghanistan, Indonesia, Bangladesh, Sudan, Chechnya, Somalia and many other countries where all attempts are being made to adopt that perfect model that is applied in Saudi Arabia. It is redundant to mention that the Taliban movement in Afghanistan was a perfect embodiment of Wahabism. Taliban is still alive and strong despite the presence of Allied forces in Afghanistan. ISIS is another realization of the Wahabi dream.

So what is so peculiar to Wahabism? Muhammad Ibn Abdel Wahab (b. 1703-d. 1792) was a reform movement leader; but contrary to our Western term of reform, Abdel Wahab regarded reform as a transition backward in time in order to take up "the same life style of the early simple Islamic society of the first century of Islam. Anything added to Islam is a heresy, a fad, a trend, a craze that is not becoming of true Islam." Therefore, Abdel Wahab set the principle that absolutely every idea added to Islam after the middle of the third century of the Muslim calendar or era (early tenth century CE) "was false, against true Islam" and hence "should be eliminated."

Abdel Wahab wanted Muslims to adopt and solely adhere to the original practices and beliefs of the Quran and the prophet Muhammad. In addition, for Abdel Wahab, Ibn Taymiyyah, Qutb, and Abul Ala Maududi, there is clear distinction between a true Muslim society and a *Jahili* (infidel, apostate, ignorant, or pre-Islamic) society. In other words, a society is either true Muslim or not Muslim at all.

It is noteworthy to mention at this point that Wahabists do not like to be called "Wahabists" or just followers of Ibn Abdel Wahab; they rather prefer the term *Salafists or Salafis* which means adherents to the early Muslims who lived at the time of the prophet Muhammad. "*Salafists*" literally means "fundamentalists."

Among the many fads Abdel Wahab considered dangerous to faith were visiting tombs and graves, frequenting burial places of the dead, whether of one's relatives or of *Aowliyaa* (Muslim Saints), men wearing gold, making sacrificial offerings, and all that he considered superstition. Ibn Abdel Wahab considered these practices inappropriate for true Muslims.

Moreover, women should not show any part of their bodies at all. Men and women should be separated at all times except if they are members of the nuclear family only. Hence, a man cannot see or talk to his sister-in-law for example. A male teacher cannot see his female students of any age.

Therefore, for contemporary advocates of Wahabism, art, literature, democracy, cinema, science, technology, coeducation, educating women, modern fashion, etc. are not going to be part of a true Muslim society. All forms of modernism, enlightenment, creativity, or secularism are considered heretical, unorthodox, and sacrilegious to Islam.

Abdel Wahab emphasized extreme religious devotion and outward piety such as the dress code: for men, a short garment that should be five inches above the ankle (it is a horrible infraction if the garment reaches the feet; no reason given why it should not reach the feet other than the prophet Muhammad wore his garment so; the ankles have to be visible at all times), men should grow a beard like the prophet did (even though all men even before Islam grew beards), women should cover completely from head to toe.

Moreover, exaggeration in piety and Quran citations must fill one's talk on any subject all the time. Quran-peppered conversation is a sign of faithfulness and devoutness. One must use the prophet's sayings and prayers in all occasions to show his or her adherence to Wahabism. For example, when one enters the bathroom, one must pray and recite what the prophet used to say. Moreover, one has to take practice to extreme to prove his or her conformity to Sharia of Allah; otherwise, a shadow of being less of a true Muslim may be cast on him or her and that could incur negative consequences to that individual.

If one does not perform these duties and practices, then he or she lives in a state of *Jahilyyia* (this word refers to pre-Islamic barbarism, a state in being an infidel or a state of apostasy and ignorance).

The word *Jahilyyia* literally means ignorance and it is used to describe any state or society that is not following the strict application of the Quran and Sunnah. That applies equally to both a pre-Islamic society and to a modern secular society.

The danger of this distinction by Wahabists is three-fold:

1- Any modern society is condemned and it is legitimate to battle and destroy that society if it does not apply the Sharia of Allah. It is a society that is "Jahili" according to extremist Wahabists.

2- Equally disturbing is that any individual deemed to be not conforming to the Sharia of Allah is also doomed and can be killed licitly and legitimately since he or she is not a "true Muslim." This makes all people according to Wahabis and radicals living today of any religion or denomination who are not applying Sharia of Allah a legitimate target to be liquidated.

3- A true Muslim will be generously rewarded by Allah when he or she punishes the enemies of Sharia of Allah or those who oppose it.

These are very disturbing and all that the world has witnessed in the last thirty years of Islamic terrorism proves that Wahabi and radical doctrines are live and working in establishing a state of terror to rule the world.

Wahabism is Abdel Wahab's Utopia, a Utopia of regression, of degeneration, retardation, alienation, disaffection, isolation, estrangement, rupture, falling backward, distrust, disconnection, extrication, and introversion. It is a serious psychological malaise that infects a whole society in the name of religion.

The echoing question is why Wahabism and Islamic extremism are a concern. The answer is very simple:

1- Wahabists and Muslim extremists are bent on using violence and all forms of militancy to spread their Islamic "Utopia" in the whole world to save it.

2- Wahabists and Muslim extremists are planning to take over the whole world. To them, it is a sacred duty to spread "Sharia of Allah" and establish an Islamic state in all corners of the universe. It is silent terrorism as they also use deceptively peaceful means and tactics in infiltrating the West.

These threats are no joke. They are very somber and real and should be taken seriously by the free world. No one will be safe from those extremists and every day passes, the free world is closer to a dismal destiny under the rule of scowling Imams and sullen Mullas.

No wonder that Osama Bin Laden was a Saudi Wahabist; all his followers are. The attackers of September 11 were all

Wahabists, fifteen of them are Saudi while the other four were Egyptian and Emirati.

There are radical voices in the Muslim world that try to cover up the rise of Islamic extremism by calling Western attempts to stop terrorism as "Islam bashers." These strident voices call the West Islamo-phobic only because the West tries to protect itself. These radical voices in the Islamic world are a kind of smoke screen that tries to blind us and shut us up while terrorists are preparing for their next attack on Western targets. It would be very naive and moronic if we in the West crumble under such browbeating from terrorist propaganda and extremist lip service that just numb our senses. Moderate and peaceful Muslims who are the majority of Muslims are against radical and Wahabi vicious goals.

The Jewish and Christian alliance is crucial to stop this trend in the history of mankind. Similarly, an alliance with Hindus, seculars, and moderate peaceful Muslims is crucial to curb the gloomy end of humanity at the hands of terrorists. It would be the end of human civilization that evolved for so many millennia and I hope it will remain intact for our children.

The danger is real. The Muslim fundamentalist Abul Ala Maududi said clearly that:

"Islam wishes to destroy all States and Governments anywhere on the face of the earth, which are opposed to the ideology and programme of Islam regardless of the country or the Nation which rules it."

He also unashamedly adds (which I quoted before but I repeat these words again to emphasize the danger):

"In reality, Islam is a revolutionary ideology and programme which seeks to alter the social order of the whole world and rebuild it in conformity with its (Islam's) own tenets and ideals."

So Muslim fundamentalists are intent on taking the world and there is no joke about that. We see they are taking it inch by inch and they have to be stopped sooner before it is too late.

"Every sign in the world we see today is a step towards the inevitable takeover of the world by Muslims, Insha'a Allah," one Muslim cleric named Sheikh Hazim Abu Ismael (b. 1961) claims. He further claims that "Everything has set the preconditions for the deterministic Islamization of the world." For radical Muslims, everything that is not Islamic or not according to Sharia is not worthy to exist and should not exist in the first place. "It is only a distraction by the devil to test good Muslims, but Allah's will and resolve will prevail at the end and the whole world will be Muslim. It is Allah's determinism that Islam will be the only religion in the world," Abu Ismael says. The Quran is fraught with evidence, radicals affirm, that supports such claim.

Having said that and having collected all this evidence, I call on the civilized world to unite against Islamic radicalism. There should be no conflict between Capitalism and Communism; there should be no conflict between Chinese economic interests and American interests; there should be no clash between Latin America and North America; there should be no friction between Russia and Western Europe;

there should be no apprehension on the part of Africans or Asians toward the rest of the world. There should be no trepidation on the part of moderate peaceful Muslims who are actually the majority of Muslims to unite with the rest of the world to fight terrorism and radicalism that are hurting them first. There should be no tension among all societies of the civilized world. There is one danger to the whole world: Radical Wahabi extremism. I call on moderate Muslims to join the West, and I know they are ready to take that step, but, unfortunately, they are tremendously apprehensive of retaliation from extremists.

All present-day terrorist groups such as Boko Haram, Taliban, the Muslim Brotherhood, ISIS, Al-Qaeda, Islamic Jihad, etc. are waiting to take over any time. They are ready to deliver their services of terror on the demand of their leaders to destroy the world. They are spreading out around the globe and striking roots wherever they settle, east and west, north and south.

Chapter Fifty

The Last Lecture

I remember the first class I taught in Saudi Arabia. It was a drama course and I taught Shakespeare among other dramatists. I also remember the students' objection to Hamlet's famous line "to be or not to be." and how that started a firestorm of criticism since the ideas were considered anti-Islamic and promoted individual free will.

Today I am giving my last class and coincidentally most of the students in this class are the same of the first class. Three years and a half are in between. From freshmen and sophomores to seniors about to graduate in few weeks. They grew up a lot, mentally and psychologically. They are different and to put them to the test, I asked them how Shakespeare sees mankind as free and not controlled by fate or any hidden powers.

"We humans have the right to be or not to be," Khalid said.

"We have the right to be the way we want," Al-Shahri said.

"Humans can reject the despise of office," Abdullah said.

"Or despotic rulers," Ahmad added.

"No to abusive clerics," affirmed Hani.

"Fate is not more powerful than humans," Mustapha said happily as if he broke free from extensive fear.

"We are not like flies in the hands of wanton boys," Al-Shahrani said.

In *King Lear,* another great play by Shakespeare, one character affirms that the Gods cannot seal our fate or make us like flies in the hands of stupid people.

"We can choose our way and shape our minds and our lives," Aamer said.

Then I asked about this passage:

"As flies to wanton boys are we to th' gods,
They kill us for their sport."
(King Lear, Act 4, scene 1, 32–37)

"We will not accept it to be controlled by ignorant clerics who use us for their fun and profit," Hatem said firmly.

"How about these lines," I wrote on the board.

"The fault, dear Brutus, is not in our stars,
But in ourselves, that we are underlings."

(Julius Caesar, Act 1, Scene 2, 140-141)

"We need not blame others if we accept our fate because it will be our fault. We, humans, have free will and a rational mind to use," Hazim said loudly and with his hands fisted.

***

"Good boys. I hope to see you soon somewhere in this big universe. So long."

That was my last lecture in Saudi Arabia.

Shakespeare was a great philosopher as well as a great writer.

He summed up a lot of wisdom in his plays. He helped me a great deal in my mission.

He told us about our life today. Many of his plays decode history and we can read and understand modern-day events as Shakespeare shed light on them in his plays.

I was so proud. I knew I did my job well. I felt goose bumps all over my body, and I was about to cry out of triumph and happiness. There is hope in the land of Muhammad where soon the light will cover every inch in it and then it will expand beyond and all over the Islamic world and rid it from its ignorance, radicalism and bigotry.

The time I flew westward out of Saudi Arabia for the last time was early morning, and I could see sunlight had spread on the eastern side of the Hejaz Mountains. The other side was in complete darkness. However, I knew the light would cover the other side soon and spread all over the Islamic world.

Chapter Fifty-One

A Case of Mistaken Identity

A horrible incident happened to shy courteous Professor Yehya. A Saudi woman accused him of touching her in the supermarket, a grave offence in Saudi Arabia like in any other country. But being not so outwardly religious and married would make his punishment a terrible one. Why does it make a difference when one is married? I was told in a sketchy narrative that a married man or woman involved in a sexual offence receives far more punishment.

So I went to a local Saudi lawyer and we tried to figure out how to defend professor Yehya.

When I asked for the security video, the security officer first denied there was a security system installed. When I told him I could see cameras all over the supermarket, he claimed the system is fake, a dummy one, so to speak and only serves as a deterrent. So I had to come up with a trick. I told Yehya I had to cook a little scheme, so I returned after two days and I first claimed I lost an item I purchased but I did not find it when I got home. I demanded a refund or a replacement. Strangely, one of the security personnel took me to the security room. We walked through a dark long hallway. It was a very scary place and from a panoramic glass window on the second floor, I could see the whole store. There were more than twenty-four TV security screens. The guard asked me about the receipt; he checked the date and time. He scrolled back the recording to the specified date and time that was marked on the receipt and he rolled forward the tape and I could clearly see myself and the bagger putting items in plastic bags. The security guard even played the tape on slow motion mode with zooming mode. I insisted that not all items purchased were bagged. After a little argument, I told him then that was fine. Then I looked at him and opened the issue of the case. He was silent for a while, a long while or what seemed to me an eternity. I offered him money. He shook his head and asked for more details about the case. I explained to him how difficult my friend's situation was and how desperate we were for evidence.

***

In less than twenty four hours I had a copy of the store security video of the 5:12 pm of April 29, 2012. The video clip duration was twenty-nine minutes from the moment Yehya entered the store to the time he left. The accuser was always visible and at no moment Yehya came close to her or even walked in the same aisle where she was. She actually was on a collision course with another man, probably because she could not see him in her veil. She brushed against him and they both sprang backwards. However, the other person she brushed against had completely different features, complexion, gait, and height from Yehya. It was clear she walked towards him without seeing that man coming to her too. At the same moment they collided, Yehya was three aisles away and he was bending to pick a grocery item from a lower shelf. When he stands up, he scratches his head. The video also showed her about twenty-seven seconds later going to a security guard and pointing at Yehya while he was stepping from a completely different aisle from where she came, instead of pointing at the other man who brushed against her even though they looked completely different and dressed differently. The security personnel stopped Yehya and had him arrested on the spot.

Yehya was ecstatic when I saw him in jail few days after. His lawyer, on the other hand, did not seem half happy. We really did not understand why but I felt that he wanted to work without help from me even though he was very indifferent to the case at times. He simply did not want someone else to take the credit, so to speak.

"You could ruin the film," the lawyer said.

'What do you mean *ruin*," I objected.

"The people in the supermarket could have hidden it," he shifted.

'How could they hide a security clip that is deleted automatically every six months without any human interference," I said firmly.

"Well, it could be deleted by error," he said in a very disgusted manner. Can you stop doing anything now?" he said arrogantly.

"Don't worry. I have a copy and there is a copy on Youtube, so it will never disappear, Sir," I said defiantly. Only then he stopped arguing and promised in a low tone that everything was all right now.

***

"It was an act of man, not God that saved you and the video," I joked with Yehya. Some man could tamper or hide altogether the security videotape, the only evidence that saved him from horrendous fate.

I joked with Tim too wondering what it would be if it was him. He would be like Dr. Aziz in the famous incident of the Malabar Caves as narrated in the memorable novel by E. M. Forster, *A Passage to India*. "Dr. Aziz was a native and the accuser was an English woman," Tim noted to me. "He had a better chance defending himself," he added. I reminded him that India was under British rule and occupation at that time. I called Tim "Dr. Aziz" few times. We laughed for five minutes without stopping till we had tears streaming from our eyes and he started to cry.

The court date was not far away and Professor Yehya remained in jail all that time, about three weeks. The day was so hot and everybody was sweating. The court was half dark except for a light above the judge. The accuser was dressed in black and she was the only woman in the courtroom. She sat alone for a while. Then she was joined by a relative, probably a husband or a brother who stared at me and then at Yehya and then at me again.

The justice system in Saudi Arabia has all the trappings of a Western legal system in terms of a judge, a prosecutor, arraignment, summons, etc., but the code is all Islamic. The judge had a very thick long beard, very fat, but had a cheerful face. Yehya's lawyer went straight to the prosecutor and told him of the security video clip. When the prosecutor looked at the flash drive, he started yelling at the lawyer. Yehya and I were about to collapse.

***

The judge heard the argument and called them both towards him. He ordered his secretary to play the video privately on his computer and then called the accuser and asked her if she was the person in the clip. She said "I do not know. I can't see clearly." So the judge turned the screen more towards her on his high bench and asked her loudly but assuredly if she was that woman. She said affirmatively "Yes." During those few seconds, my heart was pounding so loudly and violently. I believed Yehya was in a worse condition. When he asked her if "the man in the cage right there was not the man who came to you," she cried and said she was confused. He let her go instantly without prejudice.

I told the lawyer who was about to sit down to ask the judge to apply the law of the Quran that punishes anyone who falsely accuses another without merit or evidence. The lawyer smiled sardonically at me and walked away. Yehya raised his hand without enunciating a word. I looked at the lawyer in the half-lit courtroom. The judge told Yehya to go without any prejudice as well after the paper work which took another four distressing days in jail.

Three weeks after the court day, Tim was sick and tired. He decided to leave as the end of the semester was due in two days. I accompanied Tim to the airport and wished him good luck. He thanked me for everything. Professor Yehya was also there. When the time came for me to leave few days after, Yehya was also there and thanked me a lot for bringing up the issue of the security camera to his lazy, slow-brained lawyer. I just told him how I knew about the security camera. It was one time when I left in the supermarket some folder that my daughter and I bought for her school and when I went back to the store, a security officer took us to the security monitoring screens room and reviewed the tape at the specified time and date on the receipt and found where the folder was left.

When Tim arrived at JFK airport in New York and was about to board his plane heading to Columbus, Ohio, he told me in an email that airport security asked him to strip completely for suspicion that he had some explosive device on him after he told the customs officer that he had just returned from Saudi Arabia. I facetiously replied, "Welcome to America."

Chapter Fifty-Two

Gains and Losses

My stay in Saudi Arabia was a very dreadful, frightful, emotional, joyful, and an intellectual venture. I met people I never thought I would meet or know in my life. I even never thought such wonderful people existed. I also saw treachery and ignorance, like everywhere else in our world. I was entertained by many wonderful incidents and encounters with amazing folks, and I was equally shocked by many terrible events and individuals. I went through a great deal of agony and also through plenty of cheerfulness. It was an ordeal, but also it was a joy. Most importantly, I gained a great deal of knowledge about Islam and Muslims.

I felt proud to have helped my dear friend, Yehya, to avoid a terrible disaster and an appalling injustice. It was just illuminating to me how justice and injustice exist side by side in the world, in the West, in the East, North and South alike. I could say there is no justice or injustice; there is only a perception of either one, sometimes, a false one.

I was equally proud of helping my students change some of their stances and attitudes towards the West and people of other religions, and for helping them perceive cultures other than the Islamic culture in a positive way. As much as I learned from them, I tried to bring their attention to new horizons of the truth about our human life, our concepts of religion, and our perception of both.

I am particularly proud of my students, namely, Sultan, Majid, Mohammad, Tahir, Ali, Shakir, Abdullah, Hajid,

Mostafa, Abdel Mijeed, Abdel Latif, Khalid, Aleneezi, Hadi, Muhie, Mahdi, Alsubaihan, Zahir, Hudieb, Alsadhan, Samir, Aakil, Maher, Wasel, Aamer, Taufik, Salih, Salah, Nayef, Saied, Soliman, Salim, Saad, Alsobeh, Sabbah, Alghamdi, Sammer, Shalhob, Fahd, Kolieb, Abdel Aziz, Rizg, Bandar, Matar, Nour, Faisal, Rakan, Waleed, Althobeit, Wael, Soaudi, Marwan, Abdel Rahman, Ahmad, Sakhr, Sagr, Badr, Hajir, Seleem, Feleh, Barak, Alotebi, Daifallah, Ashahab, Fatahi, Ibrahim, Alanzi, Aaed, Almutairy, Taihan, Alshohrany, Aiman, Masoud, Khalaf, Zahrani, Zuheir, Malki, Almalki, Hazim, Rashid, Sahli, Suhaib, Sahil, Abdel Rasheed, Hamid, Wala, Falah, Algasry, Aleisa, Abdel Mohsin, Algahni, Alnuseiry, Nagah, Alazmy Alnushiry, Yasin, Alsomiri, Alduhein, Aabir, Jabir, Alasmari, Aldukheil, Naeem, Esery, Aaser, Samid, Sabir, Abboush, Madany, Someid, Soeib, Maddallah, Alasmary, Awad, Osman, Ghazy, Aahd, Alamry, Qubesy, Alseleem, Abdel Kereem, Albilwy, Kais, Nasser, Meshaal, Alwaheby, Farhan, Aldeib, Yazeed, Alzibany, Samy, Nimr, Obeid, Aldiab, Hasan, Alatwy, Harby, Alharby, Jabr, Husein, Omran, Hany, Shafei, Aziz, Hamoud, Talal, Bakheit, Tarig, Masheib, Miflih, Dabsh, Dubaish, Fayez, Thamer, Hisham, Fadil, Algarny, Jarallah, Nawaf, Salamah, Abbas, Aowwad, Hamam, Hamid, Mosaed, Anwar, Mansour, Fahhad, Mahmoud, Abdel Hady, Mashary, Adel, Suheiman, Mousa, Fawaz, Alebesy, Farag, Misfer, Mihanna, Attalla, Amin, Almohsen, Ismael, Zeid, Shaher, Mogbil, Khamis, Almahmoud, Bagir, Maatoug, Jalal, Hijjy, Rayan, Raed, Ayob, Mosayer, Hamza, Monis, Hatim, Yousif, Abdel Hakim, Hashim, Bashir, Dosary, Hazzaa, Faris, Omar, Amr, Rakan, Shaiban, Shaaban, Ghoneim, Ghanim, Nayel, Mizhir, Nadir, Maziid, Basim, Terky, Abo Elsaood, Nasr,

Misalim, Aayed, Manahy, Alfoheid, Hassan, Hamdan, Gaafar, and many more.

***

I know for sure these wonderful men will never fly planes into buildings or kill someone just because he or she is not a Wahabi extremist Muslim; I know these wonderful intellectuals will never discriminate against someone from another religion, denomination, or nationality. It was not me who changed those brilliant students as much as it was William Shakespeare, Alan Paton, George Bernard Shaw, T. S. Eliot, Ernest Hemingway, S. T. Coleridge, Scott Fitzgerald, Edgar Allan Poe, Ralph Emerson, Henry Thoreau, Nathaniel Hawthorne, Herman Melville, Nasr Hamid Abu Zayd, Walt Whitman, Mark Twain, William C. Williams, D. H. Lawrence, John Steinbeck, Toni Morrison, Arthur Miller, Anton Chekhov, Fyodor Dostoyevsky, Robert Browning, Plato, Victor Hugo, Marcel Proust, E. M. Forster, Taha Hussein, Virginia Woolf, Al-Tauheedi, Nathaniel Hawthorne, Jane Austen, Al-Dimashqui, Leo Tolstoy, W. H. Auden, Bin Kammounah, Francis Bacon, Albert Camus, Avicenna, Emily Bronte, Chinua Achebe, Al-Farabi, Joseph Conrad, John Keats, Gibran Khalil Gibran, William Wordsworth, Al-Tayeb Salih, John Locke, G. W. F. Hegel, William Blake, John Bunyan, Al-Asfahani, Christopher Marlowe, Alexander Pushkin, Averroes, Tennessee Williams, Badr Shakir Al-Sayab, Socrates, Aristotle, Henry James, Edward Albee, Rabindranath Tagore, Emily Dickinson, Ibn Ishak, Ibn Hisham, William Faulkner, Eugene O'Neill, Geoffrey Chaucer, Gabriel Garcia Marquez,

Abu Al-Qasim Al-Shabbi, Franz Kafka, John Milton, Oscar Wilde, W. B. Yeats, Charles Darwin, Naguib Mahfouz, Andrew Marvell, Yousef Idriss, John Donne, Al-Faitory, Alexander Pope, John Keats, Thomas Wyatt, Salman Rushdie, Alfred Tennyson, Henrik Ibsen, Charles Dickens, James Joyce, Ezra Pound and hundreds of other great writers and thinkers who made life meaningful for humanity. They presented the truth to humanity without deception or trickery as politicians and the clergy do. They spoke of the truth without seeking benefits or fearing despots. They are the true prophets and gods. They saw what others could not see in this big universe. They have carried the shining light for humanity to see the truth that many amongst us here on this planet still refuse to see or unwaveringly fail to see.

***

I am so excited today after four years away from home as I am landing at Miami airport. I remembered the first day I landed in Saudi Arabia and the taxi ride from the airport to the hotel. I remembered my first meal and the first night I spent there. I remembered my first class and how challenging it was. I remembered the dean's scowling face whenever I was reported to have crossed the line in my pitch to explain a poem or a novel. I remembered Yehya's plight and what could have happened and how it ended well. I remembered my trips in the desert and to tribes' leaders seeking the truth about Islam and the Quran. I remembered the fear in the eyes of men who had evidence that proves the falseness of the Quran.

Now, I see the blue Atlantic Ocean from the plane's window and then the Florida shoreline. I could feel that life was sweeter and the world was a bit safer despite the flight attendant's announcement that there would be a hurricane brewing over the Atlantic and might hit Miami in few days and that a new spate of the 2012 presidential election debates were well in the offing. However, there were also on the plane, a Muslim man with a big thick long beard and his wife dressed in black; she was all covered up. They had their five children with them. They were completely silent. It was getting late and I feared that darkness and decay and death would hold illimitable dominion over all.

Copyright © April 2013

Table of Contents

Chapter 1: In the Land of Muhammad 5
Chapter 2: Literature and Islam 7
Chapter 3: A Conversion to Islam Event 9
Chapter 4: Faith VS Reason 14
Chapter 5: Muslims 23
Chapter 6: Islamophobia 27
Chapter 7: The Rise of Radical Islam 33
Chapter 8: Islamic Inquisitions and the denigration of other Religions: Heinous Crimes Against Humanity............................40
Chapter 9: The Quran and Its Charm 50
Chapter 10: An Empirical Study of the Quran's Charm and Power 72
Chapter 11: Waraqah Ibn Naufal 82
Chapter 12: Waraqah's Quran VS Uthman's Quran 90
Chapter 13: Reform and Enlightenment by Muslim Philosophers and Intellectuals...99
Chapter 14: Sharia and Breast Feeding......................113
Chapter 15: The Suspicion of Praying to another God............115
Chapter 16: An Australian's Torture and Sharia:.....................117
Chapter 17: Blasphemy 121
Chapter 18: Sharia and Seductive Eyes 125
Chapter 19: Chairs and Sins 128
Chapter 20: Sexual Imagination and Social Repression.........130
Chapter 21: Sharia and Legal Infanticide 131
Chapter 22: Egypt and Saudi Arabia Relations 135
Chapter 23: Saudi Arabia and Iran 142
Chapter 24: Saudi Arabia and Iraq 146
Chapter 25: Saudi Arabia and the West 149
Chapter 26: A Wife Murder and a Robert Browning Poem......152
Chapter 27: The Arab Spring (Or Is It?)....................156
Chapter 28: A Flood Disaster: A Testimony of Islamic Faith...158
Chapter 29: *Adventures of Huckleberry Finn.*.......................... 165
Chapter 30: Logical Fallacies and Dogmatic Islamic Theology169
Chapter 31: The State of Freedom in Saudi Arabia 173
Chapter 32: Travelling with Two Wives 176

Chapter 33: Car Drifting and Saudi Politics..............................182
Chapter 34: A Political Crackdown and Our Fears....................187
Chapter 35: Some People Know the Truth about Islam.............189
Chapter 36: William Carlos Williams - No Text Is Sacrosanct..191
Chapter 37: The Rime of the Ancient Cameleer and the Quran.197
Chapter 38: Reading History from Literature: Can Literature Decode Our Times……………………………………………………...199
Chapter 39: Religion VS Literature..206
Chapter 40: Faith 209
Chapter 41: Why Are Freethinkers, Intellectuals, and Religious Freedoms Important? 213
Chapter 42: Sharia, Politics and Women Drive Ban 218
Chapter 43: The State of Saudi Women in Particular and Muslim Women in General 221
Chapter 44: Can Muslim Women Play Sports? 226
Chapter 45: Democracy in Saudi Arabia 229
Chapter 46: Who Rules Saudi Arabia? 231
Chapter 47: The Legitimacy of Illegitimacy 233
Chapter 48: Wahabism and Political Islam 237
Chapter 49: Wahabism: Silent Terrorism, Islamic Determinism, and Terror on Demand………………………………………….......243
Chapter 50: The Last Lecture 251
Chapter 51: A Case of Mistaken Identity..................................254
Chapter 52: Gains and Losses 260

Visit: Samibenjamin.com
Email: samibenjamin@yahoo.com

REFERENCES

- *Al-Asfahani, Abu Al-Farag (2002). *Kitab Al-Aghani*. Dar-Sader. Beirut.

- Al-Bukhari (1997). *Sahih Al-Bukhari*. Al-Shorouk. Cairo.

- *Al-Dimashqui, Uhanna (2001). *Al-Haratiqah*. Al-Oloum. Damascus.

- Al-Farabi (1962). *Al-Madina Al-Fadila*. Dar Al-Shurouk. Lebanon.

- Al-Ghazali (1981). *The Incoherence of Philosophers*. Dar Al-Maaref. Cairo.

- *Al-Qurtobi Exegesis* (1982). Dar Al-Islam Publishing, Cairo.

- *Al-Tauheedi, Abu Hayan (2001). *Al-Isharat Al-Ilahiyah*. Al-Oloum. Damascus.

- Averroes (1961). *The Incoherence of The Incoherence*. Dar-Sader. Beirut.

- Averroes (1971). *Kashf Aan Al-Manahij*. Al-Shorouk. Lebanon.

- Averroes (1972). *Fasl Al-Maqal*. Al-Shorouk. Lebanon.

- *Bin Kammounah, Saad Bin Mansour (1971). *Tanqueeh Al-Abhath Fee Al-Milal Al-Thalaath*. Beirut.

- Corbin, Henry (April 1993). *History of Islamic Philosophy*. Liadain Sherrard (trans). London and New York: Kegan Paul International. ISBN 0-7103-0416-1.

- Fakhry, Majid (2007). *History of Islamic Philosophy*. Holland.

- Hussein, Taha (2002). *Pre-Islamic Poetry*. Al-Shorouk. Lebanon.

- *Ibn Hisham, Abu Muhammad (1962). *Al-Seerah Al-Nabawiyah*. Beirut.

* New editions of these books have been edited to remove much of the evidence that exposes the Quran's authenticity.

- Ibn Katheer Exegesis (1981). Dar Al-Islam Publishing. Cairo.

- Ibn Kodama (1962). *Al-Moghny.* Al-Shorouk. Beirut.

- Kramer (ed.), Martin (1999). *The Jewish Discovery of Islam: Studies in Honor of Bernard Lewis.* Syracuse University. ISBN 978-965-224-040-8.

- Lewis, Bernard (1994). *Islam and the West.* Oxford University Press. ISBN 978-0-19-509061-1.

- Lewis, Bernard (1996). *Cultures in Conflict: Christians, Muslims, and Jews.*

- Momen, Moojan (1987). *An Introduction to Shi`i Islam: The History and Doctrines of Twelver Shi`ism.* Yale University Press. ISBN 978-0-300-03531-5.

- Mubarkpuri, Saifur-Rahman (2002). *The Sealed Nectar: Biography of the Prophet.* Darus-Salam Publications. ISBN 978-1-59144-071-0.

- Najeebabadi, Akbar Shah (2001). *History of Islam.* Darus-Salam Publications. ISBN 978-1-59144-034-5.

- Nigosian, Solomon Alexander (2004). *Islam: its history, teaching, and practices.* Indiana University Press. ISBN 978-0-253-21627-4.

- Smith, Jane I. (2006). *The Islamic Understanding of Death and Resurrection.* Oxford University Press. ISBN 978-0-19-515649-2.

- Tausch, Arno (2009). *Muslim Calvinism* (1st ed.). Rozenberg Publishers, Amsterdam. ISBN 978-90-5170-995-7.

- Tausch, Arno (2009). *What 1.3 Billion Muslims Really Think: An Answer to a Recent Gallup Study, Based on the "World Values Survey". Foreward Mansoor Moaddel, Eastern Michigan University* (1st ed.). Nova Science Publishers, New York. ISBN 978-1-60692-731-1.

- Walker, Benjamin (1998). *Foundations of Islam: The Making of a World Faith.* Peter Owen Publishers. ISBN 978-0-7206-1038-3.

www.ingramcontent.com/pod-product-compliance
Lightning Source LLC
Chambersburg PA
CBHW081352040426
42450CB00016B/3410